THE
ART OF GUN
ENGRAVING

THE
ART OF GUN
ENGRAVING

CLAUDE GAIER
AND
PIETRO SABATTI

Translation by ANTHEA Languages

Gunmaker's Workbench.

CONTENTS

- *6*   Field Shooting and Hunting with Hounds
- *12*   The Evolution of Hunting Arms
- *22*   Decoration of Hunting Arms
- *33*   The Renaissance (1500-1650)
- *47*   The Baroque through the Empire (1650-1820)
- *77*   The 19th Century
- *105*   The 20th Century
- *121*   Portraits of Engravers
- *156*   Glossary
- *158*   Index

FIELD SHOOTING
AND HUNTING WITH HOUNDS

The rules that govern hunting have been significantly changed and refined over the course of time. Treatises on the art of the chase dating from Antiquity, medieval narratives, and artistic representations of this ancient practice reveal the evolution of an activity that, vital though it was in the beginning, has gradually become a social and sporting event. Without delving into the mysteries of a codified and multifaceted art, we must keep in mind that in Europe the hunt has been considered a feudal right since the Middle Ages and has therefore been reserved, formal exceptions aside, for the aristocracy. Apart from notables and peasants who occasionally benefited from special dispensation on certain lands, the art of the Nimrod was that of the nobility, at least until the end of the Ancien Régime and in some cases much longer.

Although he had little enthusiasm for hunting, Napoleon I insisted on maintaining the tradition of the great royal hunts as held in the reign of Louis XIV. Scene from a painting by Carle Vernet (1758-1836).

Museum of Hunting and Natural History, Paris. Former collection of the Princess of Faucigny-Lucinge.

Some practiced it with such passion that they devoted themselves to it several times a week or even daily. The monarchs set the example in this regard. It is reported that Louis XIV of France, usually anxious to attend all sessions of his Council, dismissed his ministers one February day in 1685 to abandon himself to the pleasure of kings. As if by way of justification, he sang to himself, "Nothing can stop him when he's called by the hunt" to a fashionable tune by Lully. And it was said of his great-grandson Louis XV, when he wasn't hunting: "The king does nothing today." That is more or less the sentiment that Louis XVI wanted to express on July 14, 1789, when he wrote in his diary, "Rien." Not from a lack of understanding of the events in the Faubourg St. Antoine, but because he returned from the hunt empty-handed. According to Madame Campan, Marie-Antoinette's secretary, hunting was "the only passion Louis XVI ever developed."

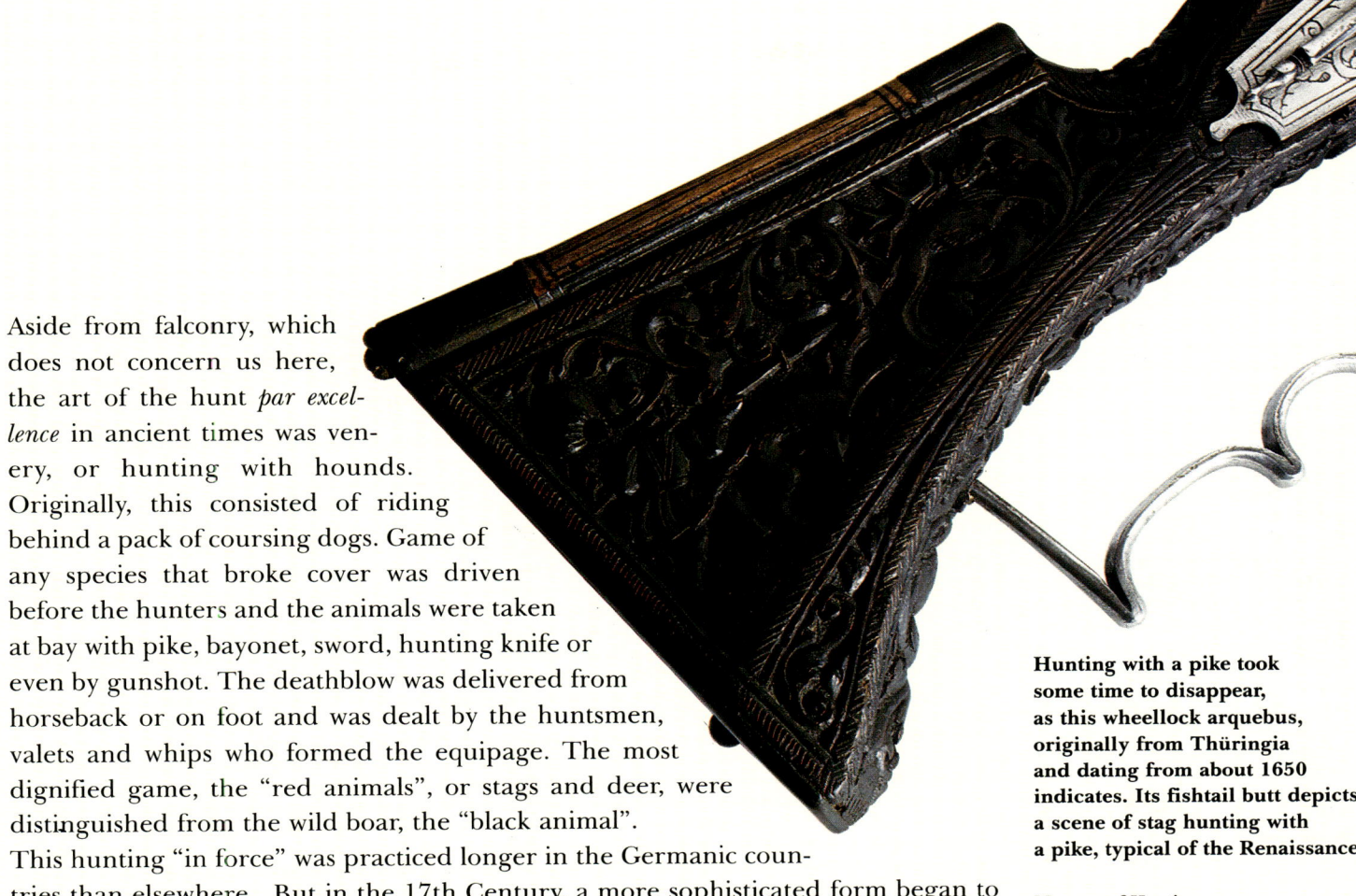

Aside from falconry, which does not concern us here, the art of the hunt *par excellence* in ancient times was venery, or hunting with hounds. Originally, this consisted of riding behind a pack of coursing dogs. Game of any species that broke cover was driven before the hunters and the animals were taken at bay with pike, bayonet, sword, hunting knife or even by gunshot. The deathblow was delivered from horseback or on foot and was dealt by the huntsmen, valets and whips who formed the equipage. The most dignified game, the "red animals", or stags and deer, were distinguished from the wild boar, the "black animal".

This hunting "in force" was practiced longer in the Germanic countries than elsewhere. But in the 17th Century, a more sophisticated form began to evolve in France—hunting with hounds for a single animal selected in advance, a mode that was eventually to spread everywhere.

The "drive" enjoyed extraordinary popularity in the 17th and 18th centuries. Its principle is simple: the beaters "start" the game and funnel the prey into a "chute". There, hunters are hidden in a blind armed with pikes or bows, crossbows or, later, firearms. These princely hunts, called "hecatombs" or "houraillemens" in Old French, were practiced avidly and with great splendor in the German and Italian courts and to a lesser degree in France, where the estates of Marly-le-Roi, Saint-Germain-en-Laye, Fontainebleau and Compiègne sometimes hosted these somewhat unsporting extravaganzas. These possibility of escape was even slimmer, the animals having first been herded into a corral, then driven between flags and nets into open country or even forced to cross expanses of water under the fire of huntsmen stationed in stands. These conditions led to some fabulous hunting paintings.

Hunting with a pike took some time to disappear, as this wheellock arquebus, originally from Thüringia and dating from about 1650 indicates. Its fishtail butt depicts a scene of stag hunting with a pike, typical of the Renaissance.

Museum of Hunting and Natural History, Paris.
Former collection of G. Pauilhac
On loan from Army Museum.

In sixty-nine years in Germany, the Electors of Saxe, Johan Georg I (1611-1656) and Johan Georg II (1656-1680), killed more than 223,000 game animals, not counting birds. In Bohemia, in eighteen days in 1753, Emperor Francis I fired 116,209 times using twenty-three rifles. His total: 19,545 partridges, 18,273 hare, 9,499 pheasants and other game, or 47,950 specimens in all.

Live pigeon shooting began to predominate in the 19th Century and there are records of 500 killed per hunter in a single outing. In the 1860s it was the turn of Great Britain to adopt the drive. Admittedly the conditions from then on were fairer, but the bags still stupefy today's hunter, more concerned with ecological equilibrium.

Louis XIII hunting stag with hounds. This engraving illustrates both hunting with hounds and the drive, which came into vogue in the 17th Century.

Engraving illustrating *La chasse royale*, written by King Charles IX, in the 1625 edition dedicated to King Louis XIII.

"Trap" shooting, at balls made first of rubber, later of glass, and launched with a catapult, appeared in the United States in the 19th Century. Its purpose was to provide shooters with intensive practice on inanimate targets. The glass balls were replaced with clay targets, and this kind of shooting has been practiced universally from the turn of the century in various forms that simulate the conditions of wingshooting.

Compared to the splendors of "venery" (which have yet to disappear), the various forms of hunting today seem less dramatic and more individualistic. Particularly since the hunting laws, which began in the 19th Century, these have almost totally supplanted the ancient forms. At this point, more modern images come to mind: the hunter-dog team, the hunter in his blind, and the "pirscheur" (a stalking hound) coming upon the game. Then there is the somewhat faded image of the "great white hunter" of exotic lands Samuel Baker, Frederick Selous, Edward Buxton and Theodore Roosevelt, to name a few.

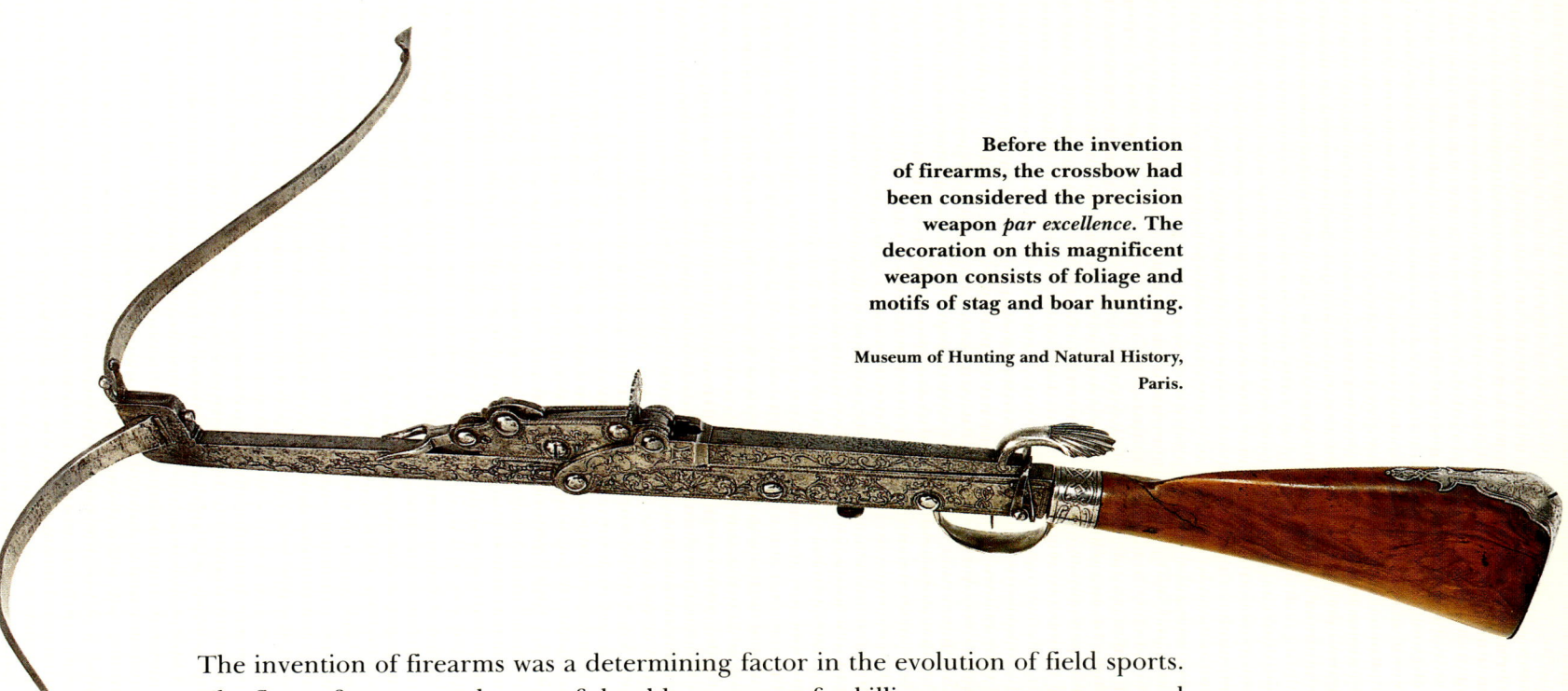

Before the invention of firearms, the crossbow had been considered the precision weapon *par excellence*. The decoration on this magnificent weapon consists of foliage and motifs of stag and boar hunting.

Museum of Hunting and Natural History, Paris.

The invention of firearms was a determining factor in the evolution of field sports. The first references to the use of shoulder weapons for killing game appear around the year 1500. In his poem, "Theuerdanck", published in Nüremberg in 1517, Melchior Pfintzing tells of Emperor Maximilian of Austria killing waterbirds with a crossbow while sailing from Gelderland to the Province of Holland at the end of the 15th Century. The same monarch is depicted killing a chamois in an illustration of the *Tiroler Fischereibuch* by Jörg Kölderer, a treatise written in 1504.

Several years earlier, in the time of Pope Alexander VI (d. 1503), Cardinal Adriano Castellesi's poem "Venatio" ("The Hunt") describes a hunting party in the Tivoli park in the presence of the Roman curia. He notes that an unfortunate hedgehog was shot by a member of Cardinal Sforza's retinue.

These references actually are rather late, considering that by that time shoulder weapons had already been used for decades for military purposes. The notion of hunting with them must have sprung quickly to mind, but various considerations probably discouraged this. First, the noise of firearms was apt to scare off the game (while the crossbow was described by a Spanish adage, "Mata y non espanta"; or "It kills but frightens not.") Then there was the copious smoke of the exploded black powder and the difficulty of using this substance in bad weather. Finally, the nobility, conservative by nature, always opposed anything new, at least initially. Whatever the reason, these impediments largely disappeared by the beginning of the 16th Century, when the use of firearms for hunting began to spread. In 1515, for example, the King of France, Francis I, issued an edict in which, among other things, he authorized gentlemen to shoot waterfowl or to have them shot on their lands. The same year in England, Henry VIII legislated against hunting deer with

Detail from a hunt with hounds organized in honor of Charles the Fifth. This painting by Lucas Cranach, dating from 1544, indicates the attitude of the nobility of the time: The favored weapons in their shooting parties were crossbows, not firearms, which were considered to be less accurate.

Museum of Hunting and Natural History, Paris. Former collection of the Princess de Faucigny-Lucinge.

crossbows or firearms in royal or noble domains. Ten years later, the same monarch authorized the guild masters of Saint George to practice their archery and to shoot game and birds. In the Principality of Liège, in 1540, then part of the German Empire, hunting "large red or black animals", as well as hares, rabbits and gamebirds, with crossbows, culverins and arquebuses, was forbidden by the authorities. The existence of edicts against poaching with firearms is a sure indication not only that they were by then widespread but that they were also to be found in the hands of people of humble origin.

In the latter half of the 16th Century, shooting scenes proliferated, particularly in prints or engravings and in the carvings decorating the arms themselves. The most famous of these representations are the work of an artist from Bruges, Jan van der Straeten, better known by his Latin name, Stradanus. After emigrating to Florence, he entered the service of Cosimo de' Medici and prepared "cartoons", or sketches for tapestries, for him in the form of pen-and-ink drawings embellished with gouache. These represent various hunting scenes that illustrate perfectly the customs of the time. These designs were engraved and later published in a collection entitled *Venationes ferrarum, avium, piscium* ... ("Hunting of wild animals, birds, fish ..."). It is interesting to note the custom, common at that time, of depicting game animals and birds at rest, or even in their lair, and not moving or in flight.

Field shooting does not seem to have been practiced before the end of the 16th Century, when the introduction of lead shot, around 1550 at the latest, undoubtedly encouraged it. Shot, pellets instead of a single projectile, in smoothbore guns gave a scattering effect.

Nevertheless, shooting birds that had been flushed or were on the wing did not become really fashionable until the end of the 17th Century. Even then, hunting large game remained traditional in the German Empire and in Switzerland, with rifled arquebuses that fired ball instead of shot.

Finally, there was the curious practice, widespread in the 17th and 18th Centuries, of shooting birds while riding on horseback, which required the rider to have an excellent sense of balance and the horse to be very well schooled and be undisturbed by the noise of gunfire.

By the end of the 16th Century firearms had a place in hunting, as shown in this engraving by Stradanus of a wildfowl hunt with muskets and dogs. In the background are ducks caught in a net in a pond.

THE EVOLUTION OF HUNTING ARMS

Mercenary armed with a fuselock arquebus. The fuselock system was later abandoned in favor of the wheellock. Engraving by David de Necker (around 1520).

Since decoration of hunting arms is by definition an art of application, it had to be adapted to the shapes and spaces dictated by the general configuration of the weapon. This varied according to the development of firearms technologies, which we need to examine to understand better the aesthetics of the subject.

Reduced to essentials, a firearm is composed of four parts: a barrel, which is a metal tube closed at the rear (the breech) and open at the front (the muzzle), and which carries the aiming devices, or sights; a firing mechanism, which ignites the charge; a stock, which carries the first two elements; and finally the mountings that complete the stock and to which the barrel and mechanism are attached.

The very first firearms used for hunting—which we will call arquebuses (they were known by various names)—consisted of a stock with a short butt, of polygonal section and quite unrefined, which was not put to the shoulder for firing but was held against the cheek, to aim. The weight of the barrel, with its thick walls, and the relatively small caliber of the ball were enough to reduce the recoil. This method of aiming weapons, equipped with a butt of this type, would persist up to the 18th Century for some wheellock carbines of German or Eastern European origin.

As for loading, this was via the muzzle, a procedure which would remain the rule without exception until the beginning of the 19th Century. The powder charge, carried in a small container (powder flask) by the shooter, was at first simply poured into the barrel; the quantity became standardized when measuring

12

French arquebus, fuselock, 16th Century.

Museum of Hunting and Natural History, Paris.

**Wheellock arquebus from central Germany (about 1660-1670). The wheellock became the most popular ignition system in Germanic countries. Instead of a lighted fuse, it relied on a clockwork mechanism to create a spark through friction.
This type of weapon was not held at the shoulder for firing but against the cheek.
This method of aiming would persist until the 18th Century in some wheellock rifles from Germany.**

Museum of Hunting and Natural History, Paris.
Former collection G. Pauilhac.
On loan from Army Museum.

nozzles became more common. Then the shot or ball was tamped down over the powder with a rod, and the whole was secured with wadding of cloth, paper, leather or simply moss from a tree. Then a little fuse powder was placed in the receptacle, called a powder pan, which surrounded the aperture drilled in the rear of the barrel. Firing was by means of a fuselock, that is to say a plate inlaid in the stock, in front of the grip, which consisted of a hinged metal arm, the serpentine, holding in its jaws a lighted fuse. When the trigger was pressed, the serpentine and its fuse were lowered towards the main pan, firing that powder which, in turn, via the aperture, fired the charge, which expelled the projectile from the barrel.

It was discovered early on, probably in the 15th Century, that making the projectile spin in flight would stabilize its trajectory and increase its accuracy and range. This was achieved by cutting shallow grooves, called "rifling," in the bore of the barrel, which spiraled from breech to muzzle and imparted spin to the ball. In this case, to force the lead ball to "take" the rifling, while ramming it into the barrel at the time of loading, the ball was partially covered in a greasy fabric patch. This ensured a tight fit and at the same time acted as a lubricant.

The countries of the German Empire were for a long time the specialists in production of such firearms. These weapons were usually equipped with a "cheek" butt and a finger rest to ensure better hold—whether firing from the shoulder or not.

Such single projectiles took the form of spherical lead balls, sometimes hardened with antimony. These served to define the weapon according to the quantity of balls which could be cast from one pound of lead. So, a 12-bore arquebus was one that fired a ball of a diameter such that on average twelve could be made from one pound of metal.

A 16 or 20 bore meant that more balls could be produced per pound, so they were smaller. This system of sizing is still used today and international agreements set sizes

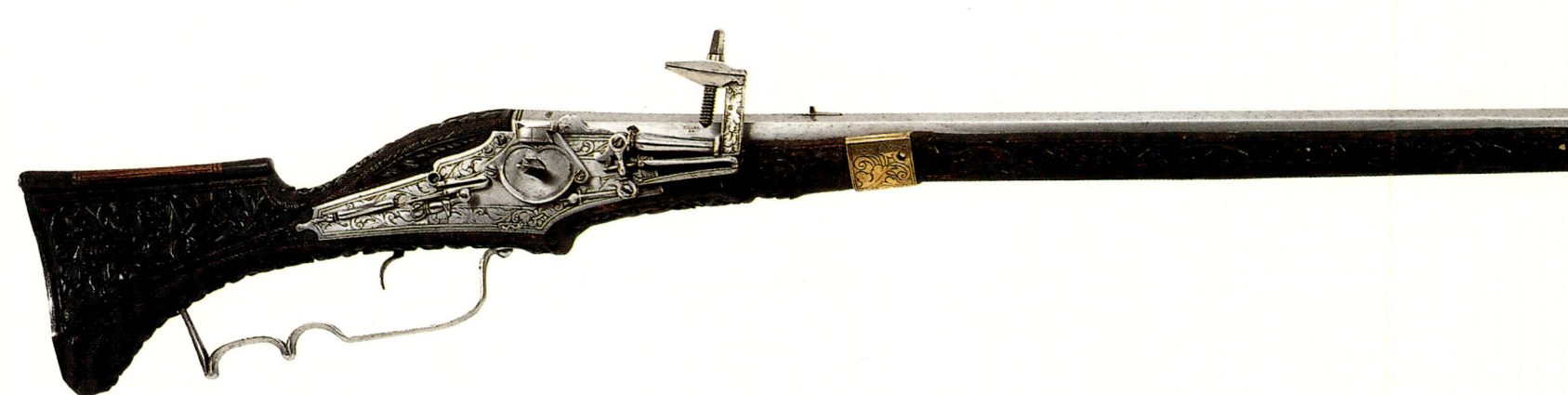

Arquebus with external wheellock dating from the 1650s, from Thuringia. The very long barrel of this arquebus allows use of powder of mediocre quality, which took longer to burn and expel the ball.

Museum of Hunting and Natural History, Paris.
Former collection G. Pauilhac.
On loan from Army Museum.

corresponding to the old subdivisions of the pound. Round balls remained in use in rifles until around 1850, when elongated projectiles—the first true bullets—were recognized and came into use because of their superior ballistic qualities.

As we have said, the first buttstocks were not shouldered. Some, indeed, which were curved backwards, were held against the chest (hence the name "pétrinal" given to weapons so equipped). However the shoulder stock appeared in the 16th Century and after about a hundred years of experiments (fish-tail butts, spiral butts, ham-shaped butts and so on) it finally settled into the form we know today.

In spite of its success, the disadvantages of the fuselock system were immediately apparent. It forced the shooter to carry burning material, visible from a long way off and easily extinguished by wind or rain. Moreover, it presented some danger when the shooter had to handle powder at the same time. On the other hand, the simplicity of the mechanism was an advantage, which explains its long life in spite of the appearance, at the beginning of the 16th Century, of rival systems. The first of these, which had already been seen in the drawings of Leonardo da Vinci, was the wheellock. It takes its name from the disk of steel, with grooves cut all around the circumference, which projected into the powder pan. This "wheel" was connected to a spring, which was wound by means of a key. The hammer was no longer a serpentine equipped with a fuse; grasped between its jaws was a piece of sulphurous pyrite. When the trigger was pressed, the hammer came down into contact with the wheel, which simultaneously began to turn under the action of its spring. The friction of the flint on the steel grooves produced a shower of sparks, which fired the fuse powder. The advantage, especially for hunting, was obvious: no more naked flame, and it was now possible to carry a weapon that was ready to fire instantaneously when needed. The wheel mechanism, which is rather complicated to make, was used largely in the 16th and 17th Centuries, and right up to the beginning of the 19th Century on some Eastern European firearms. Shortly after the invention of the wheellock, another mechanism

Detail of arquebus shown on the left. The lockplate is engraved and carved. The wheel mechanism, rather complicated to make, was used mostly in the 16th and 17th Centuries.

came into use, which, because of its simplicity, enjoyed great success until the beginning of the 19th Century: the flintlock. Here, the hammer carries in its jaws a piece of beveled flint. There is no wheel. The powder pan is covered by a bent part whose lower part acts as powder pan-cover and the upper part as the steel or "frizzen". When the trigger is pressed, the flint on the hammer hits the steel which tips the powder pan cover, allowing the spark produced by the blow to light the priming powder. There were many variations of this type in different countries. The one which we have just described is the French model, a type of lock from the which the name "fusil" derives, which was soon applied to the whole weapon.

The flints, which enabled fifteen to twenty-five shots to be fired before they became blunt, were produced in their millions. They were still being produced after 1900, for use in trade guns sold to some remote African tribes. The extraction and cutting of the flint, called "pyromaque". was largely responsible for the prosperity of the "pebblers" of Loir-et-Cher, as it was for the flint-knappers of southern England, areas known for the quality of their flint deposits and their specialized workforce.

Black powder, a mixture of saltpeter, sulfur and charcoal, which was used up to the end of the 19th Century was for a long time of variable quality. So gunmakers sometimes made very long barrels (60 inches and more) to give the powder room to burn completely and generate all its force. It was only due to progress in chemistry and ballistics at the end of the 18th Century that we have weapons of the smaller sizes that we know today.

From the beginning hunters and shooters dreamed of a repeating weapon. One that would either introduce several charges into one barrel, or increase the number of barrels. The first case involved superimposed charges, which would be fired by several hammers in succession, beginning of course with the one

Hunters' dreams came true with this double-barreled flintlock rifle with damascened barrels. The decorations are gold and silver. On the lockplate is inscribed the signature of Pirmet, the famous arquebusier who worked for the king of Westphalia, Jérôme Bonaparte, before becoming the appointed arquebusier of Louis XVIII.

Museum of Hunting and Natural History, Paris.

closest to the muzzle. Or perhaps the weapon would have magazines from which the shooter would take powder and projectiles by moving a lever when reloading. In the second case, a system of extra barrels was already known, by the German name of *Wender:* two to four barrels, fastened together, each equipped with a powder pan and a steel. By means of a button, the shooter could bring each barrel in turn into the axis of the breech and could activate the hammer by pressing on the trigger.

But in most cases, until the 18th Century, hunting was done with a single-barreled gun. In about 1730 a new technique of welding barrels together with copper or tin appeared, possibly from Saint-Étienne, the French gunmaking center. From then on, use of double-barreled hunting firearms spread—despite some reluctance on the part of shooters in various countries – and even sometimes firearms with three or four barrels, (the German "Drilling" and "Vierling"). Around 1800 the double-barreled gun became the standard equipment of the hunter.

Another innovation of the 19th Century that should be mentioned is the technique of making barrels of damascus steel. Until then, gun barrels usually were made of a strip of iron rolled longitudinally and closed by forging. To make the tube stronger, it was decided to wind the strip in a spiral around a mandrel and to improve the metal itself by amalgamating recovered products such as forged iron, horseshoe nails, and horseshoes that had already been "worked" by hammering. These techniques came

Pair of rifles for big-game hunting by Devisme (about 1835). Percussion locks and double barrels in damascus steel; lockplates and furnishings engraved with animals.

Museum of Hunting and Natural History, Paris.

from the Middle East; they were discovered on weapons taken from the Turkish enemy in 1683 at the siege of Vienna by the victorious armies. Damascus steel was continuously improved until in the 19th Century it became an ingenious mixture of iron and steel, hammered and twisted together many times to the point where it offered not only the strength necessary for firing the powders of that period but also highly valued decorative patterns that appeared on the surface of the barrels. The introduction of machine-bored solid-steel barrels did not force an abrupt end to the reign of damascus steel, which continued to be forged, in decreasing quantities, until about 1930.

The flintlock rifle worked passably well. Certainly the delay, on the order of half a second, between pulling the trigger and firing the round would surprise present-day hunters who are used to instantaneous response. They would also be astonished by how sensitive the powder was to humidity. "Keep your powder dry" was the holy law, which meant, for example, not loading the weapon too long before firing, and reloading immediately afterward, to avoid condensation in the chamber of the still-hot barrel. You also had to take great care not to inadvertently reload an already loaded rifle, a potentially dangerous error inherent in all muzzle-loading weapons where the contents of the breech cannot be seen. The phenomenon of "hang fire", that is, delay in lighting the powder, was fairly common. All these hazards were described in doggerel by the British writer Markland, in 1727, in his work entitled *Pteryplagia or the Art of shooting on the wing.* These incidents sometimes had dramatic consequences. Markland tells of a young hunter who, when his gun did not fire, thought he had forgotten to load it. He put the barrel to his mouth to see whether air blown into it would escape properly by the priming hole, as would happen with an empty

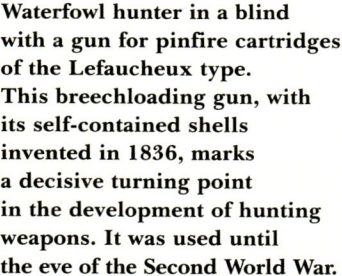

Waterfowl hunter in a blind with a gun for pinfire cartridges of the Lefaucheux type. This breechloading gun, with its self-contained shells invented in 1836, marks a decisive turning point in the development of hunting weapons. It was used until the eve of the Second World War.

weapon. In fact, it had hung fire: the shot blew his brains out…

In 1807 the Scottish pastor Alexander John Forsyth registered a patent which would, in the space of a few years, make the flintlock an antique. He replaced the priming powder in the pan with fulminate of mercury and replaced the flint hammer with a striking hammer. The blow of the hammer on a plunger, or piston, in contact with the mercury fulminate caused a small explosion, which ignited the main charge via the traditional aperture. Many improvements followed. Fulminate primer was made in the form of pills, tubes, paper capsules, or bands but the most practical, introduced shortly before 1820, was a copper capsule, which supplanted all the others. The old powder pan was replaced by a nipple over the aperture and it was onto this, where the hammer struck, that the new primer cap was placed. The transformation of the flintlock into a percussion lock proved so simple that many flint weapons were modernized and equipped with the new system. But the percussion principle did not eliminate the major inconvenience of all the systems which had preceded it: the necessity of loading via the muzzle. Certainly, breech loading was known and had been used at times since the Middle Ages. But it fell short by one important defect: locking the breech of the weapon. Perfecting a satisfactory breech closure would be the main task of gunmakers, for the first three-quarters of the 19th Century. There were countless inventions, and it would be impossible here to describe them all, but in the space of one lifetime firearms advanced from archaic equipment to modern tools that hunters still use today. The first significant innovation was that of the Swiss Samuel Pauly, who worked in Paris in the First Empire period: a firearm with opening breech, into which were put paper cartridges fitted onto a copper base, fitted with a fulminating fuse. This system was perfected by Robert in 1831.

The first rigid, one-piece cartridge that provided a satisfactory seal was probably the one invented in 1836 by Casimir Lefaucheux. In this, the primer was struck by a pin fixed perpendicularly on the base of the cartridge which was driven in by the hammer at

Double-barreled rifle for pinfire cartridges, Lefaucheux system.

Museum of Weapons, Liège.

the moment of firing. The Lefaucheux pinfire cartridge was very popular in continental Europe right up to the beginning of the 20th Century, perhaps too popular because for a long time it eclipsed another, more promising, French invention, the centerfire cartridge created by Pottet in 1855. English gunmakers were inspired by it, however, and improved their designs to the extent that in the space of one generation they became world leaders in the field of hunting arms. During the same period, between approximately 1860 and the Great War, the Americans also showed remarkable creativity in this area. This is the period when there was a great increase in the number of breechloading hunting weapons with sliding barrels and especially tilting barrels, equipped with external hammers and using modern-style centerfire cartridges. Then, late in the 19th Century came the weapons known as "hammerless", that is, with internal hammers. The English gunmakers Anson and Deeley were the first, in 1875, to produce a practical hammerless gun, to which was added an automatic ejector for empty cartridge cases. In 1856 the London gunmaker James Purdey introduced a double-barreled breechloading rifle, called "Express" to convey the power of a train. This weapon with tilting barrels fired conical balls of high caliber intended for large game, including the great Indian and African animals. For longer range but lighter use, single-shot and repeating rifles with lever or bolt actions appeared between 1860 and 1880.

**Detail of rifle shown above. The barrel, in damascus steel, another great 19th Century innovation, was manufactured by Bernard.
The engraving was by Cuvelier. Note the interlaced scroll framed by fine gold inlay, and on the trigger guard, a hunting dog in search of game. This weapon was shown in the Exhibition in Paris in 1867.**

Museum of Weapons, Liège.

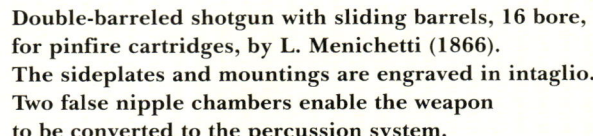

Double-barreled shotgun with sliding barrels, 16 bore, for pinfire cartridges, by L. Menichetti (1866). The sideplates and mountings are engraved in intaglio. Two false nipple chambers enable the weapon to be converted to the percussion system.

Museum of Weapons, Liège.

The introduction, from 1860 onwards, of modern gunpowders called "smokeless" brought about a noticeable reduction in bullet caliber or diameter, compensating for the smaller mass of these projectiles by greater velocity. These, which had become conical or tapered, were from then on jacketed, that is, covered by a harder metal envelope intended both to increase their penetration and to avoid fouling the barrels with soft lead.

For shot cartridges, an essential improvement of Anglo-American origin (the principle of which had been known for a long time) was adopted after the 1870s: choke-boring. This consisted of a small constriction in the diameter of the barrel near the muzzle. This concentrated the shot charge and produced a more compact grouping at longer range. Thus choke-boring enables the shotgun hunter to kill game farther away.

In spite of the existence of over-and-under barrels from the 16th Century on, the custom from the 18th Century on was to place double barrels side by side horizontally. It was only after the 1920s that over/under came back into fashion, concurrently with the side-by-side system. Today, both arrangements are widespread and both have their proponents.

Finally, in order to trace the major lines of development in hunting weapons, we must note that the first automatic, or self-loading, firearms date from the end of the 19th Century. However for sporting reasons, the popularity of these weapons worldwide

Holland & Holland Express rifle. The decoration is typical English scroll engraving (London, c. 1900).

Museum of Weapons, Liège.

does not equal that of the other, more classic models, with the notable exception of waterfowling.

In the course of this historical account, we see the pace of development accelerating, and realize that the more one nears the present day, the more numerous are the improvements and changes: there is more similarity between the arquebus of the time of François I and the firearms of the first Napoleonic era than between these and the hunting weapon of 1880. On the other hand, the shotgun and the hunting rifle have not changed very much since then. However, in the meantime, industrialization and standardization have made their mark, and firearms production is now more regulated than ever. The question now, and this will be the main point of this book, is what aesthetic benefits have come from these opportunities and imperatives, for manufacturers and shooters alike.

Shotgun with over and under barrels made by Browning for the Bicentennial of the United States. This is a replica of the gun presented to President Gerald Ford in Washington DC. The sideplate (detail above) represents the eagle and the American flag inlaid in gold.

Museum of Weapons, Liège.

DECORATION
OF HUNTING ARMS

As well inlays of as gold and silver and jewels (and more besides), a great variety of decorative techniques have been used on weapons. These can be divided into two categories, those used on metal and those on wood. Here we will describe the main techniques of both. First, to give honor where honor is due, the engraving.

ENGRAVING

Engraving involves cutting into metal in order to reproduce decorative designs on it. These may include representations of subjects, that is, people, animals or any more or less realistic images (sometimes "tableaux", or entire scenes), or simply ornaments, which may be both stylized and conventional designs, often vines and leaves. Ornaments are almost always present in engraving on a weapon, alone or to help emphasize decoration within the overall composition. Engraving of subjects is rarely used alone: it needs support and ornamental framing in order to harmonize with the parts of the weapon it is intended to embellish.

The engraver works standing up, at his or her workbench to give his shoulders and arms the greatest freedom of movement. The part he is working on is held in a vise that is rotated by a foot pedal, or in a ball vise, a heavy sphere of cast iron that can be clamped in any position. The craftsman uses a burin, or chisel, and hammer to make the incisions in the metal, or a graver, which he pushes with his hand like a ploughshare. In the first case, the line is deeper and sharper, and the nuances are obtained by retouching and additional work. In the second case, the engraver makes con-

Engraver working on his feet (for greater freedom of movement) with hammer and burin in the Beretta workshop, in Italy's Val Gardone.

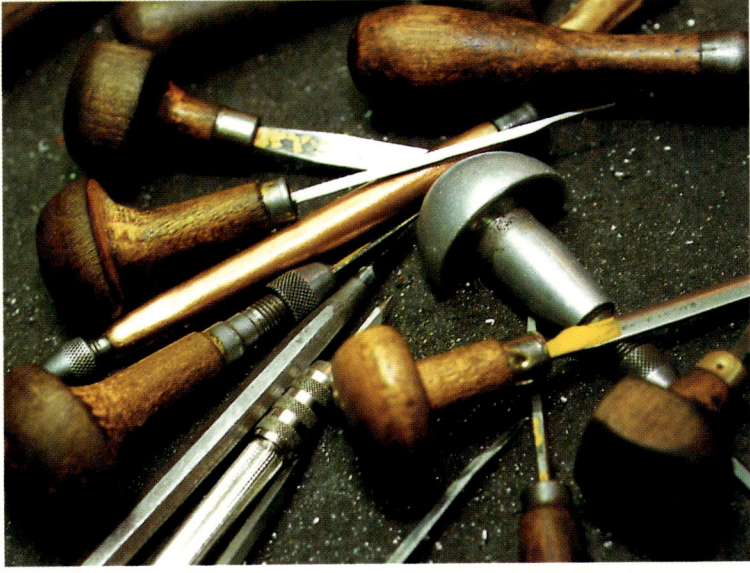
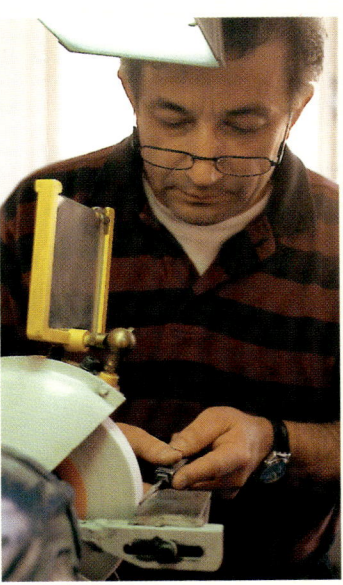

Ball vise ideal for engraving while sitting down.

Engraving tools: dry-point, burnisher, engraving burin with hammer and "bulini" (scribers), characterized by their mushroom-shaped handles.

Grinding wheel of Severino Ferraglio.

tinuous finer grooves or a succession of tiny dots, a very laborious process that gives a wonderfully delicate result, but which is not always appropriate to the vigorous style often expected on a gun.

Different instruments are also used depending on the work to be done: dry-point etching for a superficial cut, a chasing tool to deepen it, a burnisher to take out the background, a polishing tool to smooth the surface, files… Tools have been introduced to simplify some operations and gain time: the tracing wheel, which makes delicate squares to show shadows and shading; the fork, whose toothed edge cuts several parallel lines simultaneously, and the embossing punch to push back the metal.

There are many engraving techniques. The most common – but not necessarily the simplest – is copperplate engraving. This uses lines and light shadows to give all the nuances of perspective and even to give the illusion of relief. Intaglio engraving consists of cutting the designs as if for copperplate, but then taking out the background in such a way that the decoration appears to be in relief.

The essential qualities that we expect from an engraving on a weapon are the quality of the lines and of the relief of the ornaments and subjects, as well as the meaning of the composition. It is important for the work to be executed - accurately and meticulously, with passion, but it should also fit harmoniously with the surfaces that have been given up to

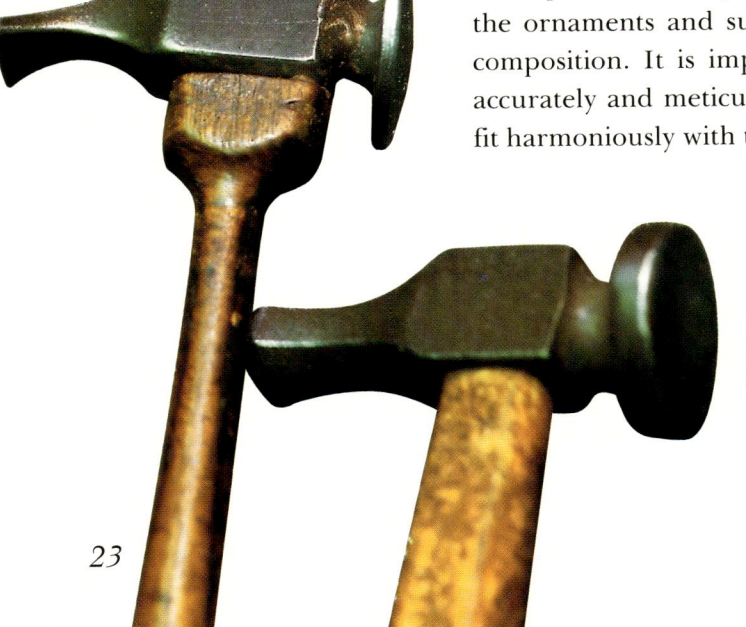

Engraving hammers used to achieve cuts of different depth.

Engraving hammer of synthetic material.

Detail of intaglio engraving by Hervé Boulay done with hammer and burin and finely shaded using the graver. With this technique, the decorative design appears to be in relief.

Copperplate engraving done with a graver on a First Empire hunting rifle. This technique, the commonest, gives the illusion of relief.

Museum of Hunting and Natural History, Paris.

it. The best engravers bring all these elements together perfectly. Then and now, however, there were certainly those who did not possess all these talents and who joined together with others who had complementary skills: some would engrave scrolls and plumes, others hunting scenes, yet another would design all the decoration and position it appropriately on the weapon. One craftsman might be content simply to copy patterns, another would combine them in different ways in order to innovate, a third would make new designs, thus showing true creativity. However, in general, such engraving and related techniques were based on the applied arts, where value lies more in the adaptation of styles and fashions than in pure creation. It is also an art of accommodation where often the craftsman only has a narrow margin to work in because of all the specifications by the commissioner of the work, who is rarely driven to be daring. Thus there is a tendency to concentrate on quality of execution, performance and amazing technical feats.

"Nature does not take leaps." Neither does engraving. It accumulates, sometimes it selects, it forgets nothing of the past. Its ornamental textbook is an encyclopedia, a store of memories that goes back to ancient Greece, even to Egypt. Anything may suddenly reappear. Rubbings of finished works, plaster casts of chasing,

Copperplate engraving in progress.

photography, the many sources of documentation today all constitute a veritable treasure trove into which engravers can dip, according to the fashion of the time. The best engraved and decorated weapons have always been displayed in museums and workshops throughout Europe and America. Today we also have richly illustrated publications as a source of inspiration for gun engravers.

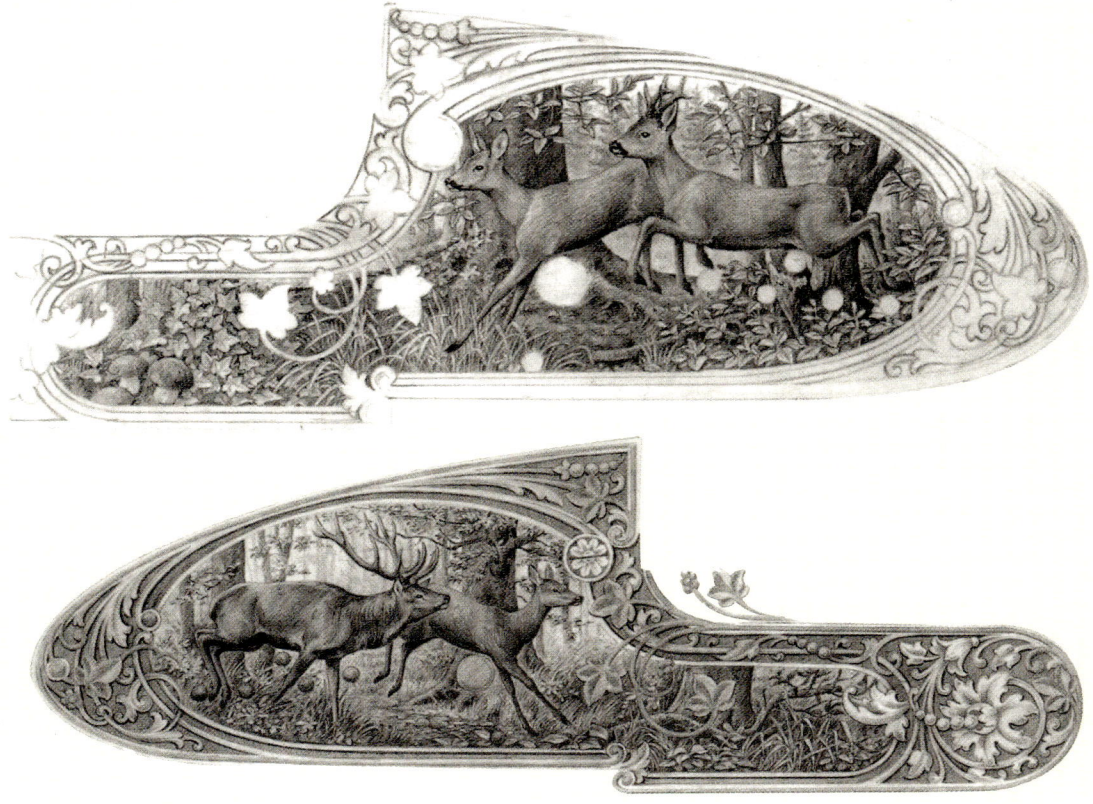

**Samples of engraving.
Ink is spread in the engraved lines to allow an impression of the whole to be taken on special paper.
This technique is also used to reproduce original engravings on copper panels.
Facsimile of engraved plates by Alain Lovenberg.**

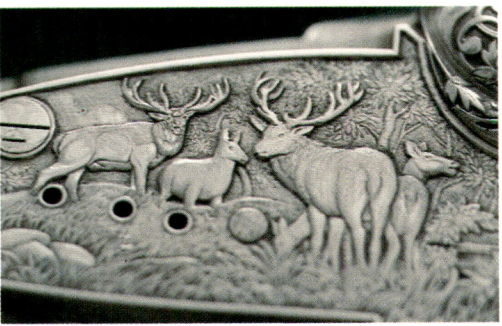

Engraving on a lockplate of a Beretta rifle. This technique provides true relief sculpture.

Etching

Introduced in Italy in the 15th Century, etching means allowing an acid to act on a metal base so as to "etch" a design there, instead of cutting it mechanically with burin or graver. The base is coated with a protective varnish into which the required decoration or composition is scribed with a pointed tool. Depending on how hard the craftsman presses on this instrument, he will only go through the coating or will go deeper and carve grooves in the metal, thus determining how deep the acid will bite. The etching, a solution of nitric acid, attacks only the parts laid bare by the tool. All that is then required is to wash away the acid, to put an end to its action, and to remove the remainder of the protective covering. The result is an engraved decoration into which much nuance and a great degree of delicacy can be obtained. Nevertheless, the action of the acid widens cuts in the metal and sometimes gives them a "smeared" appearance, so that the outlines are not as clear as those made with tools.

Chasing

Chasing is metal sculpture in relief. As the thickness of the material allows, it goes from the thinnest bas-relief to high relief and even to sculpture in the round, that is, three-dimensional designs that stand out from the background.

Inlay

The technique of inlay consists of cutting grooves in the metal base, then undercutting these grooves into a profile called a dovetail. Wires or

**Chasing on the trigger guard of a rifle by Nicolas-Noël Boutet, dating from the First Empire.
The work is in the style of Louis XVI, although the nature of the decoration foreshadows the Empire style.**

Museum of Hunting and Natural History, Paris.

Lefaucheux rifle inlaid with gold.

Museum of Weapons, Liège.

sheets of gold, silver or lesser metals are hammered into the grooves, filling the cavity so they are held in place by the beveled edges. When the metal is set flush into the groove, this is called flat inlay. If it is allowed to stand out a little, it is then called relief inlay. If inlay of a certain width is required, different techniques can be used. Either the wires are laid in separate grooves so that the precious metal, once it has been pressed into place, spreads over the surface to give the impression of a continuous area, or the craftsman engraves, in intaglio, the shapes of the decoration, dovetailing the edges and inserting into the space thus created a subject cut out to size.

Whether flat or relief, inlay must be finished off with the ordinary engraving process in order to achieve the desired nuances and detail.

By using alloys (yellow, white, red or gray gold) with other precious metals, such as platinum and palladium, shades of colors can be created. But these variations are not common and are much more frequent today than in the past.

**Three stages in the inlay technique:
a line is engraved with a cutter.
A wire of precious metal is then inserted
into this using a pusher.
And finally the inlay is finished off.**

Detail of damascening on a Pirmet fowling piece (page 16). This shotgun was made in 1810 in Paris.

Museum of Hunting and Natural History, Paris.

Damascening

Damascening involves engraving the outlines of decorations or subjects, then hatching the background so that by simple pressure a thin leaf of gold or silver will adhere to it. When this has been polished, it clings to the roughened surface of the background and remains in place.

Gilding

Gilding was formerly done by applying an amalgam of gold and mercury onto the metal. When it was heated, the mercury was eliminated and a thin coat of gold was left behind, adhering to the surface. This process, hazardous because of the vapors involved, was abandoned after the 19th Century and replaced by electroplating.

Surface Treatments

Various surface treatments are applied to weapon parts in order to change their chemical composition and therefore the physical properties of the metal, at least on the surface. It was also used to obtain various aesthetic effects.

Blueing involves heating the parts in a charcoal burner then soaking them in deer-horn oil and plant oil. This gives them a beautiful blue tint.

Quenching is case-hardening of the surface of the steel, that is, changing its outer layer to make it tougher. This involves heating the metal over charcoal in a closed vessel in contact with organic substances (powdered bone, hooves, horns or burnt leather). Then the parts are plunged into an acid solution or, after the beginning of the 20th Century, into a bath of potassium cyanide. When they are dried, the parts have a marbled appearance that varies according to the firing temperature. After about 1850 efforts were made to obtain a final deep blue tint with light blue and gray-brown marbling. If the acid marbling is removed it disappears but leaves a yellowish-gray color, like old silver, which is called gray temper or French gray.

28

French gray (old silver) on a rifle of late Empire style.

Private collection.

Blacking, used particularly on firearm barrels, is a progressive oxidation obtained by repeated applications of an acid coating. This treatment protects the part against natural corrosion and gives it a pleasing appearance. The operation can be performed speedily by a more recent method, which involves immersion in bluing satts.

These processes have developed since the 19th Century and have improved. Formerly, most metal parts remained in their natural state and were simply polished, sometimes using abrasives of progressive fineness, until a degree of brilliance and polish was obtained that was called "mirror finish" or "glass finish".

Blued and damascened barrel of a blunderbuss by Nicolas-Noël Bouter.

Museum of Hunting and Natural History, Paris.
On loan from the Louvre Museum.

CARVING

Apart from some exceptional old examples made entirely of metal, gunstocks were—and still are—generally made of wood. Since the 19th Century, walnut has become the wood of choice. It is distinguished by its toughness, density, workability, and the beauty of its grain. The grain varies according to where on the tree the wood grew: either root wood (burl walnut) or wood from the first fork, with elaborate graining, or burl walnut with a "creased" appearance, caused by natural growth, or even wood from the heart of the trunk, with the most regular but the most monotonous grain.

Stockmakers at first used a wide range of wood types: fruit trees (pear, cherry, walnut, olive), Brazilian rosewood, thuya, briar root, maple, ebony … They were not interested so much in the appearance of the woods as in their strictly utilitarian properties. In the case of luxury weapons, the stock was given special decoration to increase its value, even if this meant covering it completely. So when arquebuses first appeared their butts often were decorated all over in fabric or leather.

However, in the 16th Century, stockmakers introduced two woodworking techniques: marquetry and inlay. Marquetry involves covering, sometimes entirely, the wood with a veneer of other wood, horn or even ivory, to give it a more pleasing appearance. As in the veneered furniture of today, the most noble and luxurious materials were used to cover the most ordinary of bases. Inlay involves carving into the stock of the weapon and pushing into the cavities figures or ornaments of bone, mother of pearl, ivory, iron, copper or silver. In fact inlay was done both on the wood of the stock and in the marquetry that sometimes covered it.

From the 17th Century onwards, the wood of the stocks began to be appreciated for its intrinsic qualities, and the idea developed that it was no longer necessary to overload it with decoration or additional materials to give it value. The search for an ideal wood eventually led to the choice of walnut. This was still decorated with inlay and carving,

30

Percussion shotgun (Liège, c. 1850) with barrels of damascus steel. The stock is carved in the style of Louis XIV by Jean-Michel Tinlot of Herstal.

Museum of Weapons, Liège.

but eventually emerged the clean lines we know today. This new fashion did not become immediately widespread. In Spain in the 18th Century stocks were still often made of fruitwood, and in the Germanic countries stocks continued to be inlaid as in the Renaissance. In the 19th Century we still find luxurious carved gunstocks. These rifles were made for international exhibitions or to be presented to important people, and the stocks may be of ebony or Brazilian rosewood.

This pinfire gun was made by André Fils in Paris for the worldwide exposition of 1855. The richly carved stock shows hunting scenes.

Museum of Weapons, Liège

THE RENAISSANCE
(1500-1650)

Detail of the decoration of the cheekpiece of the stock of a wheellock gun: marquetry inlaid with bone, and an ivory inlay of a boy holding a hare, followed by a dog (Germany, 17th Century).

Museum of Hunting and Natural History, Paris.

Wild boar hunt using arquebus, engraving by Stradanus.

This engraving is one of the four hundred plates in the 1585 edition of the *Venationes*.

Wheellock gun (Munich?, 1532). Typical German Renaissance intaglio engraving.

Museum of Weapons, Liège.

The Renaissance period saw the first significant developments in firearms. All the traditional styles of decoration of weapons were altered and now bore little or no resemblance to the medieval models. The new designs were characterized by an almost immoderate taste for ornament, a sort of "abhorrence of a vacuum". Italy, which had behind it the artistic traditions and history of Rome, showed the way and took on the role of initiator in the movement. Architecture, carving and the pictorial art of the ancients were called upon: the first supplied columns, pilasters and capitals, which would inspire engravers for a long time. So we begin to see arquebus barrels decorated with longitudinal grooves and made up of round and polygonal sections, also bearing

Breechloading wheellock arquebus (Bavaria, 16th Century). Renaissance scrolling and damascening. The stock has been restored.

Museum of Weapons, Liège.

moldings or beading. The muzzles were reinforced by rims or spread in the form of capitals. Engraving and inlay on weapons also reproduced the repetitive decorations on the remains of old buildings: palmettes, Greek borders, egg shapes, olive moldings and olive wreathes, tracery, roses… Carving in the round and in particular low reliefs, cameos and coins, especially medallions representing busts of emperors, supplied a wealth of references for decorators, which allowed them to work "in the antique style".

But the great fashion of the Renaissance was that of "grotesques". This comes from the decorative designs on the murals in the *Domus aurea*, the "Gilded house" in Rome. When the remains of this former palace of Nero were uncovered, in the 15th Century, they were below ground, partly covered by Trajan's baths, which explains why they were taken at first for caves, or grottoes, hence the word "grotesque". These were a continuous series of small designs, linked by wavy lines called arabesques. There was scrolling (scrolls of twisted, entwined acanthus leaves) decorated with beaming or grimacing faces, animals, chimeras, satyrs, gryphons, bull's heads (called *bucranes*) garlanded with flowers, figures wreathed in leaves, little cupids *(putti)*, cameos and curtains. European artists copied and adapted them, repeated them endlessly and enriched them by a mixture of elements borrowed from Renaissance Italy : stylized acanthus leaves, *termini* (small columns surmounted by human figures), pillars and caryatids (support columns in male and female form), cartouches (framed plaques), "skins" resembling parchments with jagged borders, horrific masks, tracery and trophies. This genre developed especially during the second

Enlarged view of the mechanism of the arquebus shown on the previous page. The intaglio engraving of lions and Renaissance motifs is enhanced by damascening.

Museum of Weapons, Liège.

half of the 16th Century, within what art historians call Mannerism, a late phase of Renaissance aestheticism characterized by a conventional method of interpreting the knowledge acquired from the first wave of this style.

North of the Alps, the Fontainebleau school contributed widely to the formation and spread of this fashion. These artists, mostly Italian, were employed in building and decorating the royal residence of François I, and they used this method of decoration in their work. The French engraver and goldsmith Étienne Delaune (1518-1583), in his work and designs, was also instrumental in spreading these ideas among the decorators of weapons and armor, especially in Germany, where he also worked.

The use of models by craftsmen engaged in embellishing luxury weapons becomes apparent in the 16th Century. Some designs from that period, either weapons or parts of weapons already made, or plans for the making of such weapons, have survived. But mostly the decorators based their work on printed plates showing various objects decorated according to the fashion of the day, such as mythological, biblical or contemporary scenes from which they took inspiration for their own work. These came mainly from southern Germany and the Netherlands and among them were the famous prints from

Detail of decoration on the barrel of the arquebus shown on page 35: a phoenix with grotesques and trophies, and acanthus leaves.

Museum of Weapons, Liège.

Stradanus' *Venationes*. France also excelled in making and circulating collections of decoration for arquebuses from the 17th Century onwards.

It was widely recognized that the Holy Roman Empire was an early leader in firearms. The invention of firearms had previously, perhaps wrongly, been attributed to the Germans themselves. In any case they were certainly pre-eminent in this field in the 16th Century.

Germany

After the 1530s, when hunting arquebuses and pistols with wheellock and fuselock became widespread, the history of weapon decoration really begins. This aristocratic art, we must emphasize, did not apply to all weapons produced—far from it—but where it existed it can be summed up as follows: during the 16th Century, the best German weapons were generally engraved, damascened or even inlaid with gold or silver. The most common designs are arabesques, vine branches, cartouches and medallions showing gods and ancient people.

Detail of the arquebus opposite. This portrait of an unknown person is on the butt.

Detail of the arquebus shown on the left. The engraved medallion on the butt shows Cupid seated on a seahorse and blowing into a shell. Around this are dragons, birds, a hunter with crossbow, a wild boar hunter with a spear.

German arquebus with external wheellock of 1590. This smooth-barreled weapon has ivory inlay on the butt. On the plate we see a stag fleeing.

Museum of Hunting and Natural History, Paris.

The decoration on the lockplate often matches that on the barrel. Because of its shape, the hammer lends itself especially to treatment. It is sometimes represented, using engraving or chasing, as a monster covered in leaves or a sea creature covered in scales, such as a stylized dolphin. This trend continued throughout the centuries, until external hammers were abandoned in hunting weapons.

But the most spectacular aspect of long German weapons was their elaborate stocks. These were inlaid with ornaments and subjects in deer horn, sometimes colored green; at first not too elaborate and rather rustic in their style, they became more refined after the mid-16th Century. These buttstocks can be divided into two categories; those which are simply adorned with decorative designs and subjects and those which are truly narrative, unfolding a succession of scenes relating to historical events or of religious and mythological significance. The cheekpiece, usually on the left side of the butt, offers the greatest surface for decoration, but the other parts of the stock are also decorated. The facets of the stock are generally emphasized by inlaid strips of bone or brass. Towards the end of the

German fuselock musket made of parts from various periods: the stock is from 1570, the lockplate from 1590 and the barrel from 1600. The butt and the stock are inlaid with mother of pearl and ivory.

Museum of Hunting and Natural History, Paris. Former collection, G. Pauilhac. On loan from the Army museum.

century butts with fish-tail ends started to appear. These were similary decorated.

We must point out that the decoration of Renaissance weapons does not always show the most noble or delicate motifs. Trivial or erotic scenes crop up here and there in the stock inlays and the ornamentation of the metal parts.

Italy

It is paradoxical that luxury arms of the period should have left so little trace in the countries of the Renaissance. The reason is that Italy was very dependent on Germany and the Netherlands for weapons and parts as well as for such specialized work. The first Italian specimens of high quality appear at the end of the 16th Century, but they later reached a level that suggests long-acquired experience of the craft.

In the second quarter of the 17th Century a school of highly skilled decorators developed in Northern Italy, especially in Brescia. Their great specialty was chasing and they developed a mastery of the

Arquebus with wheellock made around 1650 in Italy. The entire stock is completely covered with tortoiseshell. The barrel is inlaid with silver. The lockplate is decorated with filigree showing a hunting scene with a fortified castle in the background.

Museum of Hunting and Natural History, Paris.

metal. Under their tools, hammers and lockplates were patterned in high relief or in the round, like sculpted stone; they excelled in piercing metal to look like lace. Their barrels became famous as the most beautiful, the most delicate and yet the strongest in Europe. Lazaro Cominazzo was the first in a long line of gunmakers in the town of Gardone, which was a center of these skills from the end of the 16th Century until the beginning of the 19th. The splendid royal gift made by the republic of Venice to Louis XIII in 1639 represents the pinnacle of this work. It was a matching set composed of a pair of pistols and a pair of rifles, which are now in the Museum of Arms in Stockholm. It is the work of four masters from Brescia and Gardone. If we confine ourselves here to the surviving rifle (the second has since disappeared), its barrel is finely twisted and the lockplate enhanced by an engraved border. The fittings are chased, and pierced to resemble lace, and there is inlay in the walnut-burl wood. The detail of the work is such that more than fourteen hundred holes have been identified in the sideplate, all pierced with a saw and polished with a file of the diameter of a needle!

Other regions of Italy, between Bologna and Rome, also produced remarkable firearms. From these small centers, less well known than Brescia, came beautiful lockplates and stocks artistically chased during the second quarter of the 17th Century. The "Peninsula" school continued to produce work in the same vein until the next century.

France

Relatively few French firearms from the 16th Century remain and most are pistols. There are, however, enough to indicate the existence of finely made luxury weapons. Damascening and inlay in gold and silver, engraving and chasing, bone inlay (natural or colored), mother of pearl and copper wire wood inlays were made, with exquisite taste and more restraint than in the Germanic countries. In general French Renaissance weapons and their mechanisms displayed particularly elegant lines. Massive stocks were replaced by butts that could be curved (like a pétrinal) or flared towards the base, like a fish-tail. Sometimes the buttplate was finished with a scroll. The style was that of the Renaissance, with scrolls, arabesques, acanthus leaves, grotesques and masks, a style which could be likened to that of French bookbinders of the period.

As well as Delaune's patterns for decoration in the style of the Fontainebleau school, those of the French craftsman Jacques Androuet du Cerceau and Michel Le Blon, an artist working in Amsterdam, were also popular. Gunmakers took inspiration from them and adapted their designs.

With the 17th Century there appeared in France a generation of gunmakers, decorators and engravers who entrusted the designs of their projects, their own work and that of colleagues, to printers. This fertile source was encouraged at an early stage by King Louis XIII, a weapons enthusiast who acquired a large and fine collection, which has been dispersed throughout the world. Louis XIII had probably inherited this passion; his father, Henry IV, spent much of his life as a warrior. He himself received, at the age of sixteen months, a miniature set of weapons, put on his first armor at the age of two years and nine months, and fired an arquebus for the first time at four years and eight months!

The oldest surviving decorative patterns in France are those of a gunmaker from Metz, Jean Henequin. They show hammers and stocks heavily chased with animal or human subjects as well as deep scrolls decorated with fruit and flowers in the fashion of the

Woodcut showing "the life of Monsignor St Hubert Dardeine" (of Ardennes) by Hubert Le Prévost (c. 1520).

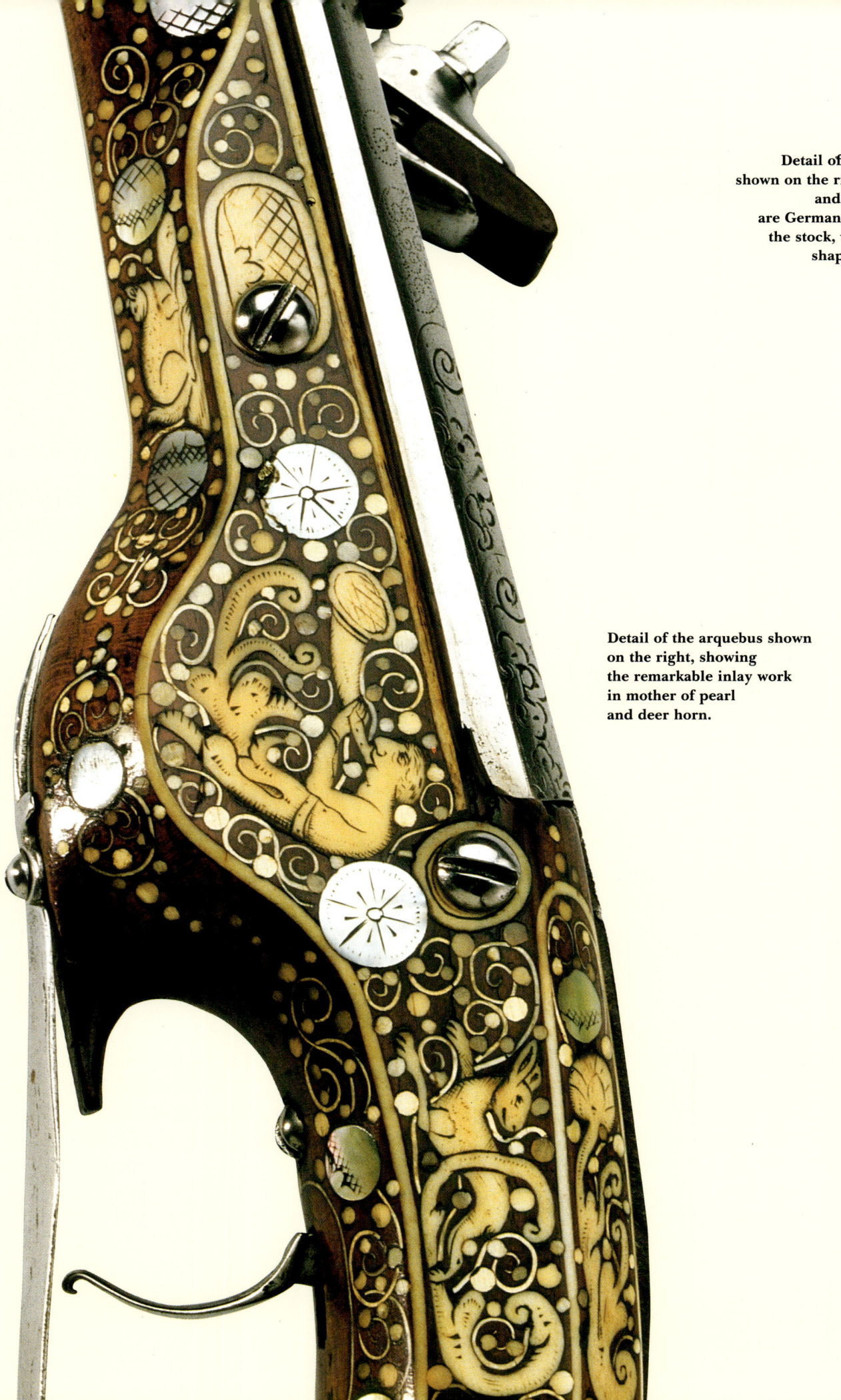

Detail of the arquebus shown on the right. The butt and the handgrip are German-inspired, but the stock, with its wheel shapes, is French.

Detail of the arquebus shown on the right, showing the remarkable inlay work in mother of pearl and deer horn.

Small hunting wheellock arquebus intended for a child. It is French and dates from around 1600. The smoothbore barrel is engraved with a punch; the stock is inlaid with deer horn and disks of mother of pearl.

Museum of Hunting and Natural History, Paris. On loan from the Army Museum.

first half of the 17th Century. In the 1630s, an engraver belonging to a family of gunsmakers, Philippe Cordier Daubigny, published a set of sixteen prints for arquebuses that combined engraving, chasing and inlay, in a heavy style mixing hunting, mythology and decoration in abundance.

Pierre (who died in 1627) and Marin (d. 1634) Le Bourgeois, from Lisieux, made pieces of exceptional quality for the king of France. Marin earned a place in the Louvre in 1608. A flintlock rifle dating from the 1620s, which is today in the Hermitage Museum in St. Petersburg, is attributed to him.

Alongside a tendency to simplify the gunstock, which was characteristic of the 17th Century, we also find many examples of stocks that are over-elaborate and barely functional until very late in this period.

The other centers of production

Luxury weapons were also produced elsewhere in Europe, outside the countries of the Holy Roman Empire, Italy and France. There were some quite remarkable variants in different countries, but none strayed far from the great artistic trends found in the main centers.

The Flemish engravers or those from Liège had influence on European weapon decorators in the 16th century due to their patterns for decoration which they created and distributed. The

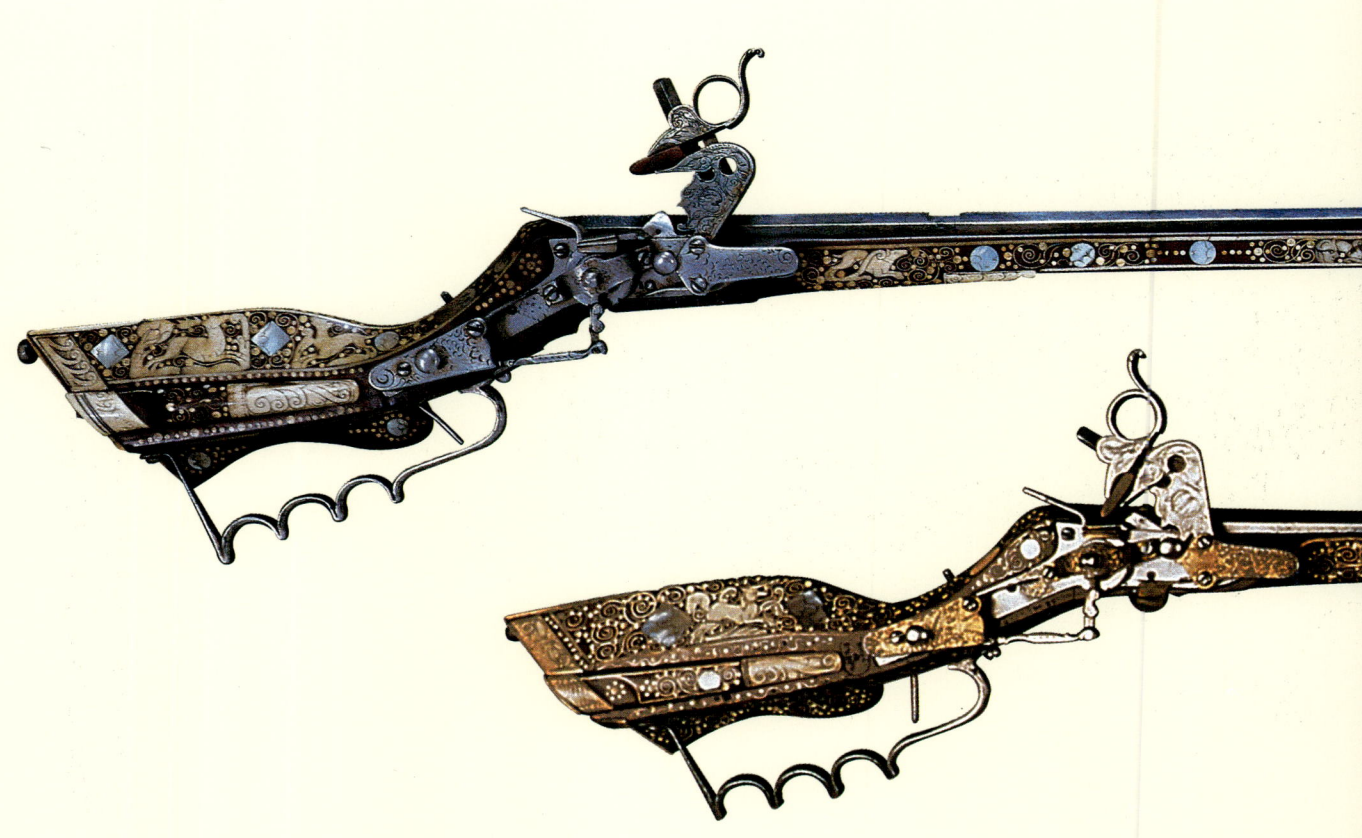

Silesian wheellock arquebus. Weapon with claw butt from the beginning of the 17th Century with plain lockplate and a hammer finely chased in a scroll design like the coils of copper springs. The stock is inlaid with bone: scrolls, decoration and small birds, all decorated with mother of pearl and deer horn.

Museum of Hunting and Natural History, Paris.
Former collection of Pierrefonds.
On loan from the Army Museum.

chasers and goldsmiths of Antwerp, such as the Sadelers or Eliseus Libaerts, taught abroad. At that time, Liège, a future great center for gunsmakers, had no luxury producer identifiable as such. However, during the second quarter of the 17th Century some weapon production is attributable to the city; these weapons were long or short, with plates and barrels chased with various subjects, especially erotic, executed in quite a rough, vigorous style, like that found in northern Europe and France on sword hilts.

The northern part of the Netherlands had become, around 1600, a great power on both land and sea. First developing their military weapons, they did not play a major part in Europe in the sector of luxury weapons. However, their craftsmen possessed all the necessary talents to meet the demands for the highest standards if necessary.

At the other extremity of the Holy Roman Empire, a completely individual category of hunting weapons appeared in the second quarter of the 17th Century. We are talking of *tschinkes*, produced in lower Silesia, in the area which today is Poland (Cieszyn, hence their name) and Czechoslovakia. These were carbines with visible wheel-locks, of small caliber for that time, with a clawed butt, intended for hunting birds on the ground. Their decoration, of a rather rustic style, consisted of scrolls engraved in outline, partly gilded, on the plate and the barrel, but especially with much inlay on the stock. These bore designs in cut and engraved horn, circles of horn and mother of pearl, as well as bands of horn or brass. The subjects are animals, monsters, horsemen and plant designs. It is thought

Tschinke from Silesia of 1620, with bone inlay.

Army Museum, Paris.

Tschinke with claw butt. On the butt inlaid with bone, a bear is attacked with a spear by a hunter helped by his dog.

Museum of Hunting and Natural History, Paris.
Former collection of Pierrefonds.
On loan from the Army Museum.

that some weapons of the same genre were produced further to the east, on the frontiers of Poland and the Baltic countries. Whether this is so or not, the decoration on the *tschinkes* shows influence of both east and west. The vogue for these weapons could have begun at the end of the 16th Century and carried on into the second half of the 17th Century.

Still in the eastern part of Europe, we must mention Russia, which had for a long time been inward-looking and absorbed with its own problems of expansion to the south and towards Asia, but which had begun, especially in the 17th century, to be more open to influences from the West. The first of the Romanovs, Tsar Michael Fedorovitch (1615-1645), founded an arms workshop in the Kremlin with foreign and Russian workers who produced a quantity of luxury firearms for the court and the great aristocrats of Moscow. The master gunsmakers succeeded in creating a style which was an amalgamation of the influences of Europe and the East. Alongside a multi-faceted personality such as Nikita Davydov, who for more than sixty years was blacksmith, sculpture and damascener at the palace for cut and thrust type weapons and armor as well as for firearms, others worked in the specialized trade of arquebusier. Their production reveals German and Anglo-Dutch influences: the plates are chased and damascened in a slightly rustic way, the butts are quite long and abundantly inlaid with horn and mother of pearl in a naïve style showing oriental influence. So the Russian arquebus developed in the 17th Century on the margin of the European artistic movement, which it joined only later.

THE BAROQUE THROUGH THE EMPIRE (1650-1820)

Detail of the rifle once belonging to Frederick I of Sweden (c. 1740), work of the German gunmaker, Adam Anton Gerhard. Eight similar weapons then to be ordered by the king as presents.

Museum of Weapons, Liège.

Frontispiece from a published collection of arquebus ornaments by the engraver Claude Simonin (1685). This was a catalog of ideas, original and already in use, for arquebusiers.

The term "Baroque" refers to an artistic style that developed in Europe in the 17th and 18th centuries. This movement sought the grandiose, the pompous, the theatrical, the pathetic and the perfection of form. The experience of the Renaissance and the values inherited from classical times were still present, but in the form of a pedestal upon which artists established a new order of thought and taste, reflecting the global society that was the foundation of their work.

France

The century of Louis XIV attracted to France, and in particular to the court, a number of foreign artists and craftsmen who combined their own work with the particularly outstanding talent already in France. The only dark cloud on the horizon was that the emigration of Protestants, as a result of the revocation of the Edict of Nantes in 1685, deprived the country of a good number of its most valuable artisans. However, this helped spread their techniques, skills and styles throughout Europe.

Books on weapons decoration continued to appear on a regular basis and were often republished. Rubbings of finished guns

Plate for the collection of arquebus designs by Thuraine and Le Hollandois (c. 1660).

Frontispiece of a work entitled *Hunting Trophies*. The illustrations drawn by C. Huet were engraved by Guélard (18th Century)

were inked and then reprinted. The circulation of these documents contributed to the spreading of the French style of weapons decoration, but sometimes with a certain discrepancy in fashion because they tended to be retrospectives. Thus the Parisian gunmaker François Marcou, in 1657, at the age of 68, published drawings of his work, from which the weapons decorator Claude Jacquinet created etchings. Thus his rather ornate style, combining monsters and chimeras with subject engravings and carved stocks, evoked the previous generation.

Born into a family of gunmakers from Lorraine, Jean Berain (1639-1711) was at first a decorator before becoming, in 1674, a designer of decoration and costumes for the Sun King. At the age of nineteen, he published (in 1659) a small collection entitled *Various very useful Pieces for Arquebusiers...* in which he presented his designs for various Parisian manufacturers. The collection had a more "modernist" appeal than the work of Marcou. Already in evidence were the rounded lockplates that would, over the course of about thirty years, supersede the rectangular plates of earlier times. Berain's collection would subsequently be republished and enjoy prolonged success. In 1660, Claude Jacquinet published another catalog of weapons that he had engraved for two "of His Majesty's ordinary arquebusiers", Thuraine and Le Hollandois (the surname of an arquebusier originally from Maastricht, Adrien Reynier), and also in all probability for twenty-four other gunmakers in the French capital, whose names he listed.

From the collection of arquebus designs by Claude Simonin. It was through these ornaments of Simonin that the Louis XIV style became widespread in European weaponry.

Around 1674, Jean Le Couvreaux, who was arquebusier to the King, published four plates of engraving designs.

At that time, the classic Louis XIV style had reached full maturity. Flintlock guns generally had octagonal breeches which, where marked by a molding, then changed into sixteen-sided polygons and ended in a cylinder with another molding as reinforcement at the muzzle. The lockplates were of rounded shape, with curved, swan-neck hammers; they were covered in engraving and chasing, executed with elegance and delicacy, in harmony with those on the barrels. Damascening and gilding were often present also. Chased iron and, on rare occasions, silver was used for the mountings. The screwplate, on the other side of the stock from the lockplate, took the form of intertwined snakes, worked in an increasingly complex fashion until, by the end of the century, it had become interlaced with medallions or subjects. The stock was long, extending almost to the muzzle. It was most often made of walnut, with an inlaid butt with a curved line profile (so-called "ham" style) or, increasingly, resembling the classic buttstock of today.

The ornaments were principally acanthus leaves, scrolls, symmetrical scallops, masks unadorned or rayed (surrounded by radiating palmleaf motifs), medallions, heads of monsters, grotesques,

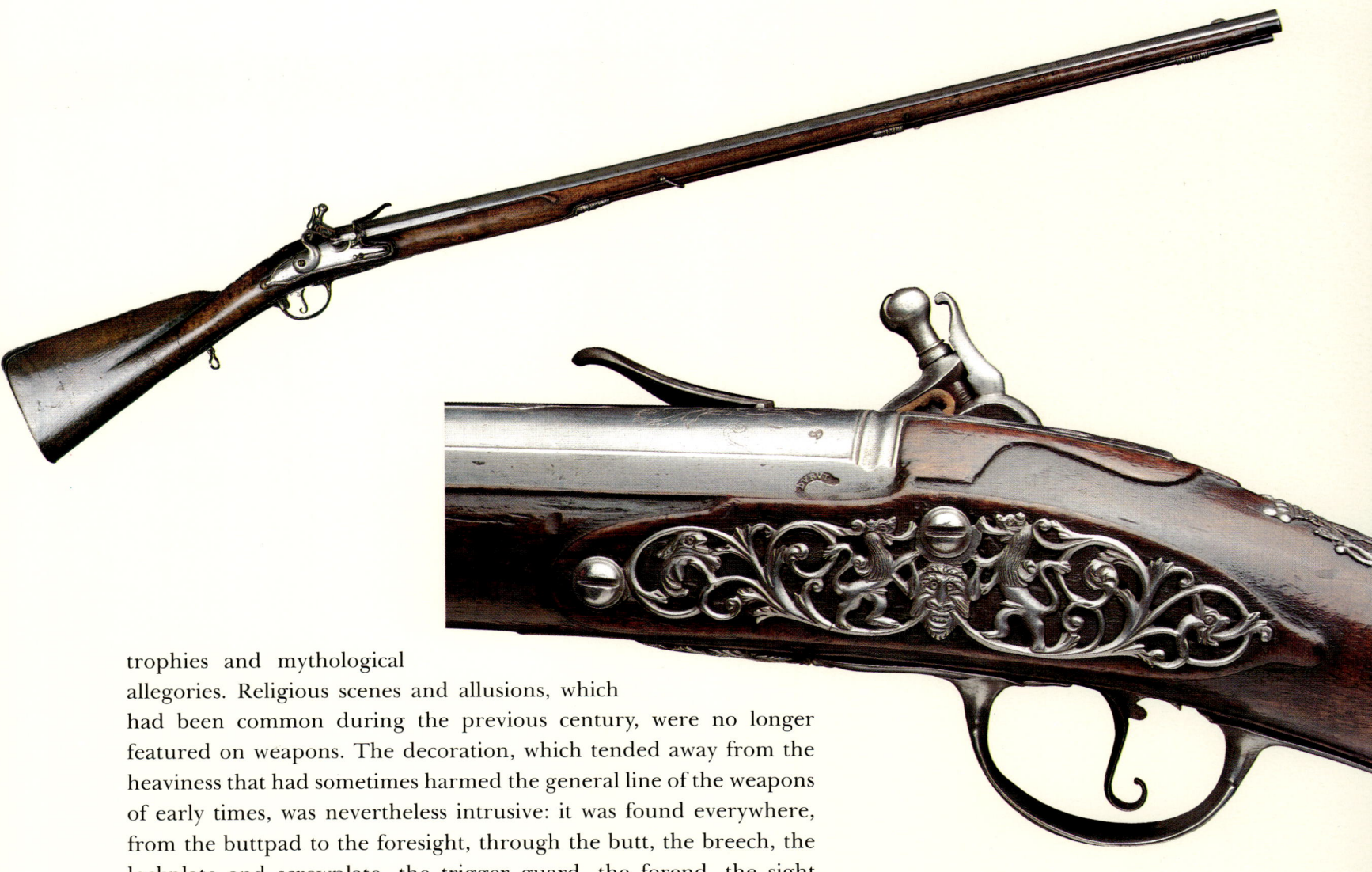

trophies and mythological allegories. Religious scenes and allusions, which had been common during the previous century, were no longer featured on weapons. The decoration, which tended away from the heaviness that had sometimes harmed the general line of the weapons of early times, was nevertheless intrusive: it was found everywhere, from the buttpad to the foresight, through the butt, the breech, the lockplate and screwplate, the trigger guard, the forend, the sight bead, and the tip of the ramrod.

Towards the end of the 17th Century, another French engraver exerted a significant influence over the luxury arquebus trade: Claude Simonin. In 1684 he published a collection of ornaments which his son, Jacques, republished nine years later. His style was more delicate, lighter, less severe and less symmetrical than that of his predecessors. Through his motifs he heralded the future grace (if not the vapidity) of the Age of Enlightenment. It was above all through Simonin that the Louis XIV style spread, belatedly, throughout the European arquebus trade. Republished in Paris in 1705, his catalog would go on to be published in Amsterdam and Nüremburg as well, in more or less the same form as the original.

During the watershed of the 17th and 18th Centuries and until halfway through the latter, other collections by gun decorators marked the development of a style that moved first through the Regency phase (which began during the latter years of the Sun King, then covered the minority period of Louis XV, from 1715 to 1723),

Single-barrel flintlock rifle from 1660-1670. The stock extends to the end of the barrel and the butt is in so-called "cow's hoof" style. The barrel is etched with a grotesque mask and the mark "Durut". The screwplate depicts a grotesque flanked by two lions.

Museum of Hunting and Natural History, Paris

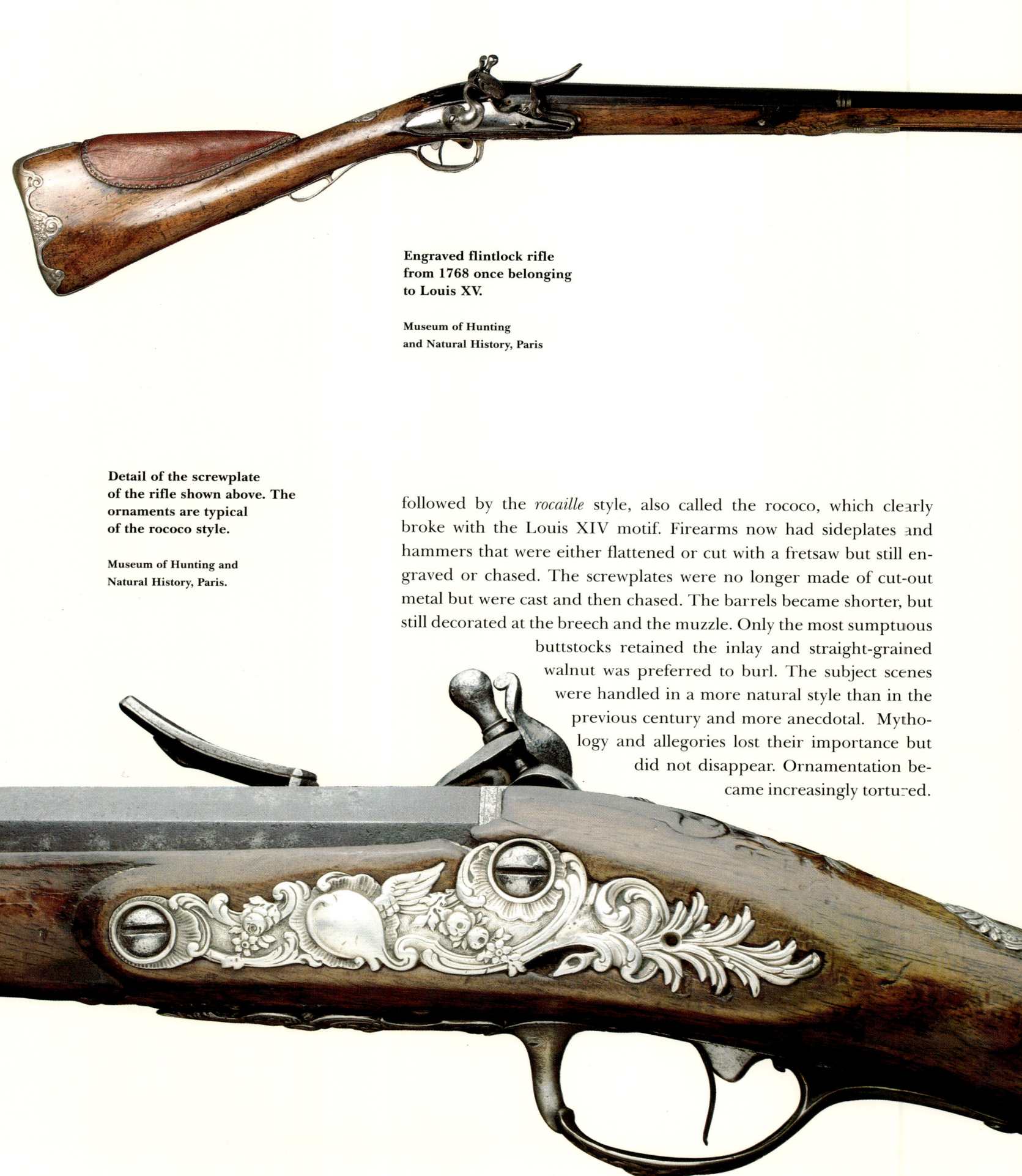

Engraved flintlock rifle from 1768 once belonging to Louis XV.

Museum of Hunting and Natural History, Paris

Detail of the screwplate of the rifle shown above. The ornaments are typical of the rococo style.

Museum of Hunting and Natural History, Paris.

followed by the *rocaille* style, also called the rococo, which clearly broke with the Louis XIV motif. Firearms now had sideplates and hammers that were either flattened or cut with a fretsaw but still engraved or chased. The screwplates were no longer made of cut-out metal but were cast and then chased. The barrels became shorter, but still decorated at the breech and the muzzle. Only the most sumptuous buttstocks retained the inlay and straight-grained walnut was preferred to burl. The subject scenes were handled in a more natural style than in the previous century and more anecdotal. Mythology and allegories lost their importance but did not disappear. Ornamentation became increasingly tortured.

Double-barrel flintlock in Louis XVI style by Joseph Frappier of Paris (c. 1770), converted to percussion towards 1835. Decoration typical of the Louis XVI style.

Museum of Weapons, Liège

Scallops with sinuous and asymmetric curves were found everywhere, along with different types of twisted and jagged shells, and scrolls in the shape of an S or two C shapes side-by-side. The collections of Nicolas Guérard (who died in 1719) and those of Claude Gillot (published shortly after 1715) remained in the Louis XIV tradition, although with a certain freedom of expression in the latter. In contrast, in the arquebus book plates published afterward by De Lacollombe, who died before 1730, the influence of the Regency style is clear. Expanded subsequently in Paris by Joseph, then by Gilles De Marteau, engravers from a family of Liège gunmakers, this collection carried the rocaille style to the peak of its popularity.

Among the most renowned craftsmen of this time were Jacques Louis Arault, arquebusier to the Dauphin of France, the future Louis XVI, and to the Count of Artois, and Jean Baptiste Laroche (who signs his name, with his son: Les Laroche), who received a license at the Louvre in 1743. Pierre Puiforcat was "first arquebusier to the King" in the third quarter of the century, and Pierre De Sainte was court arquebusier at the time of Louis XVI. Their work attests to the stimulating role played by the French monarchy in the field of artistic professions, even if they made not only luxury weapons but also the more ordinary, and more common, weapons used by most shooters. Furthermore, despite their prominence, Paris and Versailles were not the only places in the realm that were active in this field. A large number of skilled gunmakers were also working in other areas, particularly in Saint-Etienne, where the workforce, which mostly carried out ordinary commissions, knew how to produce a superior level of quality when the clientele demanded it.

Detail from the rifle shown below. On the butt is engraved the initial and crown of Napoleon.

Flintlock rifle bearing on its sideplate "Le Page, arquebusier du roi, Paris", 55 inches long and .63 caliber, with the muzzle and front sight adorned with silver palm leaves. The hammer and the base of the plate are in silver and iron engraved with foliage. The buttstock, with a silver-banded Moroccan-leather cushion, is stamped with bees and stars. This rifle, from the collection of Le Page and his descendants, is from a series executed for Louis XVI and converted around 1805 for the Emperor Napoleon I.

Museum of Hunting and Natural History, Paris.

During the second half of the 18th Century, the rococo style in France lost its popularity in favor of the neoclassical. Rediscovering the Greco-Roman world through the drawings of ancient sites and monuments—the ruins of Pompeii and Herculaneum and Etruscan remains—and influenced by England, which adopted this mode before them, French craftsmen recreated an ornamental style which was refined in comparison to the excesses and over-abundance of the rococo genre. Decorative motifs became prominent: garlands of oak, laurel and olive leaves, lattice work, ribbons, arabesques, hunting or war trophies, attributes of various professions, incense burners, bowls and so on. Copperplate engraving, depicting in particular animals and hunting scenes, was also popular, but it was overwhelmed by the ornamentation and it lacked strength and realism in itself. Gilding remained an essential finishing touch for top-of-the-range items.

At the close of the 18th Century, the general line of the French hunting arm was fine and beautiful, with or without ornamentation: walnut stock with a pad at the comb of the butt, to cushion the shooter's cheek; a short stock, and double barrels that were often made

Details of scrolls and embellishments on the side-by-side barrels of a flintlock gun by Nicolas-Noël Boutet. The richness of the damascene work is typical of the Empire style. This superb piece came from the weapons factory at Versailles around 1800-1805.

Museum of Hunting and Natural History, Paris, G. Pauilhac early collection. On loan from the Army museum.

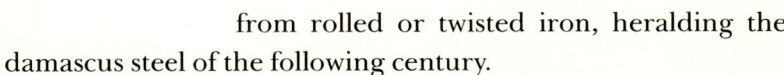

from rolled or twisted iron, heralding the damascus steel of the following century.

Far from dealing a fatal blow to the arms industry of the *Ancien Régime,* the French Revolution and Napoleon Bonaparte made it shine with an unrivalled brilliance. Above all, the latter imposed on the fine arts and decorative arts a style which both exalted him as an individual and sought references from a past as distant as possible from the "feudal abominations". In doing so, Napoleon had to revive the neoclassical trend of the late Louis XV era and of Louis XVI— while adding to it the style of ancient Egypt—as well as the splendor of deposed sovereigns, in order to hold his place among the crowned heads of Europe.

In this respect, Nicolas-Noël Boutet, who had been placed in charge of the weapons factory at Versailles, played a vital role, not only through his personal talent as a gunmaker and decorator but also by recruiting the best craftsmen in the Republic and the Empire. He also showed a desire to contribute to the ideological program of the new master of France. Boutet was clearly not the only talented person to work (or to be made to work) in this manner. Unlike other gunmakers in the country, his rival, Jean Le Page, refused to be outdone by him on a professional level. Furthermore, these "leading lights" did not deign to entrust certain tasks to well-known goldsmiths, such as Percier and Fontaine, or even Biennais.

The ornamentation of the Empire style mixed together decorative elements from classical times—such as masks, medusas,

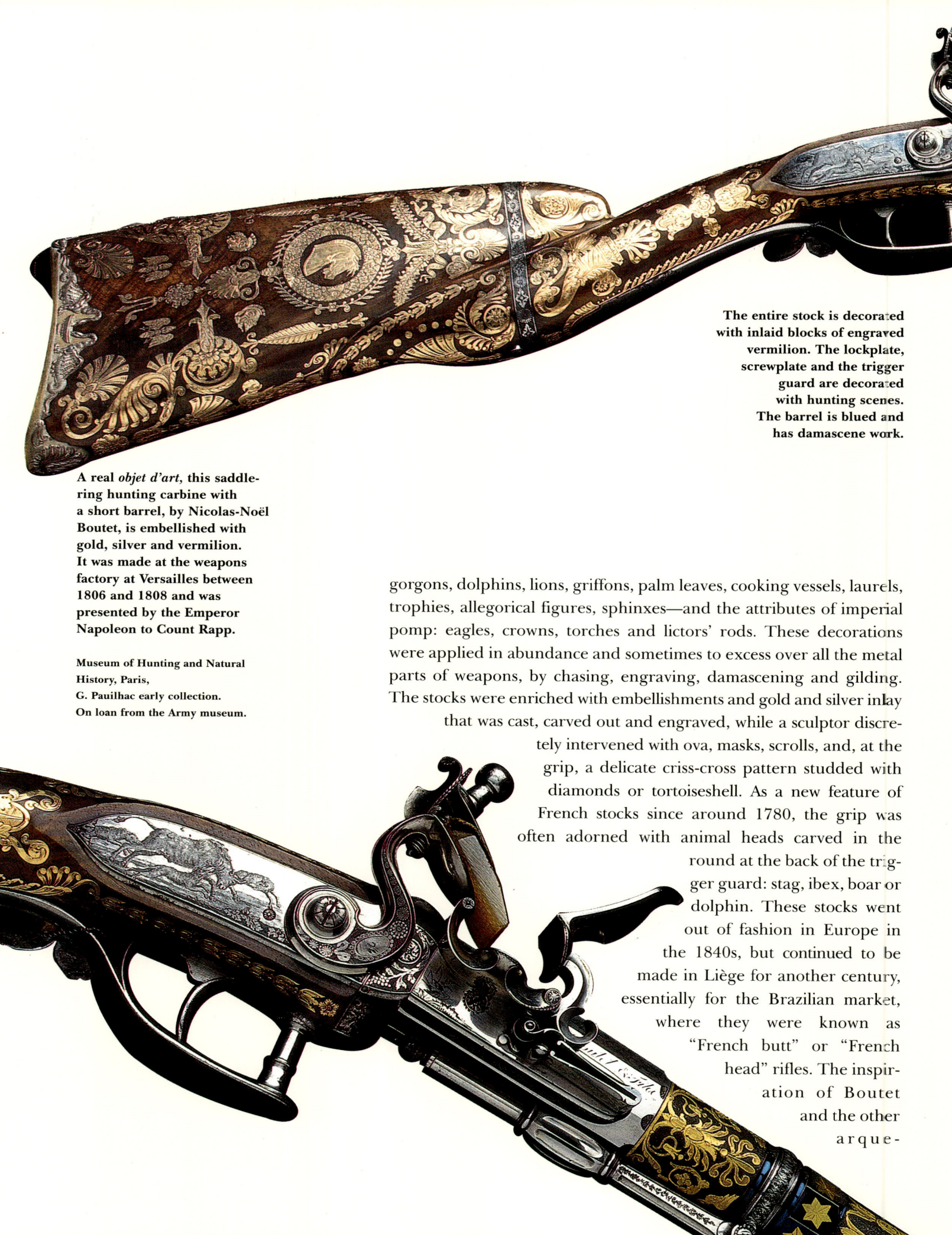

The entire stock is decorated with inlaid blocks of engraved vermilion. The lockplate, screwplate and the trigger guard are decorated with hunting scenes. The barrel is blued and has damascene work.

A real *objet d'art*, this saddle-ring hunting carbine with a short barrel, by Nicolas-Noël Boutet, is embellished with gold, silver and vermilion. It was made at the weapons factory at Versailles between 1806 and 1808 and was presented by the Emperor Napoleon to Count Rapp.

Museum of Hunting and Natural History, Paris,
G. Pauilhac early collection.
On loan from the Army museum.

gorgons, dolphins, lions, griffons, palm leaves, cooking vessels, laurels, trophies, allegorical figures, sphinxes—and the attributes of imperial pomp: eagles, crowns, torches and lictors' rods. These decorations were applied in abundance and sometimes to excess over all the metal parts of weapons, by chasing, engraving, damascening and gilding. The stocks were enriched with embellishments and gold and silver inlay that was cast, carved out and engraved, while a sculptor discretely intervened with ova, masks, scrolls, and, at the grip, a delicate criss-cross pattern studded with diamonds or tortoiseshell. As a new feature of French stocks since around 1780, the grip was often adorned with animal heads carved in the round at the back of the trigger guard: stag, ibex, boar or dolphin. These stocks went out of fashion in Europe in the 1840s, but continued to be made in Liège for another century, essentially for the Brazilian market, where they were known as "French butt" or "French head" rifles. The inspiration of Boutet and the other arque-

Detail of the carbine shown above. "Glass finish" steel with copperplate engraving of hunting scenes.

busiers came from a variety of designs: those from the period of Louis XIV and Louis XV, the hunting paintings of Jean-Baptiste Oudry, the collection of arquebus ornamentation by Augustin Dupré of Saint-Etienne and those of J-F Lucas, engraved by Renneson (around 1807-1808) and others.

The craftmanship of the weapons of Boutet and Le Page, to cite simply the two best-known, reached unrivalled heights. They were active at the peak period for flintlock weapons, the most recent improvements to which, introduced in Great Britain, were immediately adopted in France. As for the percussion lock, which had also come from across the Channel, it also experienced its first European development at the time of the Empire. The manufacture, the finishing—in particular the "glass finish"—and the fitting of the items represented perfection, both in the visible parts and equally in those hidden from view. The decoration, even if the overabundance was sometimes regrettable, demonstrated an outstanding mastery of materials and techniques.

There exist, in numerous public collections, luxury weapons signed by the master arquebusiers of the Napoleonic Period. Notable among these is a splendid hunting carbine, with a detachable barrel, signed by Boutet and Son at Versailles, which was given by the emperor to the general Count Rapp in 1808 (Paris, Army museum, on loan to the museum of Hunting). The plate is engraved with a hunting scene, the barrel is blued and damascened and the stock is entirely decorated with inlaid blocks of engraved vermilion, one of which represents a horse's head.

Detail of the carbine above. An inlay of a block of engraved vermilion decorates the stock of the carbine. It depicts the head of a horse, an allusion to the name of its owner, from Alsace. (In German, *Rapp* means "black horse".)

Arquebus with internal wheellock by Kaspar Zelner, gunmaker in Salzburg and Vienna in the early 18th Century. The butt is carved and the mountings are of gilded brass.

Museum of Weapons, Liège.

The Germanic countries

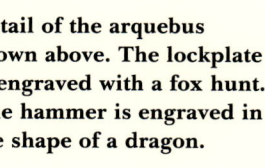

Detail of the arquebus shown above. The lockplate is engraved with a fox hunt. The hammer is engraved in the shape of a dragon.

During the 17th Century, the Germanic countries lost the domination that they had exercised over European weaponry during the previous century. The heterogeneous character of the geographic regions that made up the Hapsburg Empire, on the one hand, and the absence of a single, permanent capital, along the lines of Paris, on the other hand, acted to curb the centralizing impulse necessary for a worldwide promotion of the manufacturing arts. Furthermore, these factors increase the difficulty of covering, in broad terms, the combination of different decorative styles that were becoming evident. We will therefore limit ourselves here to the major trends and the key individuals who promoted them.

Generally, between 1650 and the beginning of the 19th Century, the Holy Roman Empire was characterized by substantial conservatism in the types of weapons manufactured and in their decoration, and by the profound and progressive ascendancy of French design.

Conservatism meant that until the end of the period covered here, these regions remained the major producers of wheellock guns, even though the flintlock dominated everywhere else. Moreover, most of these arms were fired, as before, at the cheek and not from the shoulder. There was also a strong inclination to decorate them as they had always done. Hence the continuation of horn inlay in the buttstock, even though this material was increasingly replaced by engraved blocks of iron or brass. Brass especially became popular for inlays because it readily withstood gilding and also was more malleable and

Detail of the arquebus above. The screwplate depicts a hunt for wild boar and hare.

more amenable to being engraved. Also evident was an appreciation of the value of natural wood for the stock, without veneer, although it meant using (or even sometimes abusing) appliqués. Chasing never disappeared but was replaced, especially on the plates of wheellock weapons where there was a large surface available, by engraving or by etching, which was often of a very high quality in contrast to the somewhat scanty, all-purpose scrolls of the previous period. The themes were hunting-related or borrowed from the wars with the Turks (even on hunting weapons), which were familiar to the populations of central Europe at that time.

Whereas in Munich, Vienna, Prague and elsewhere in Bohemia, wheellock arms decorated in the rococo style were produced up until the middle of the 18th Century, the style originating from France did not begin to penetrate the Germanic countries until the end of the 17th Century.

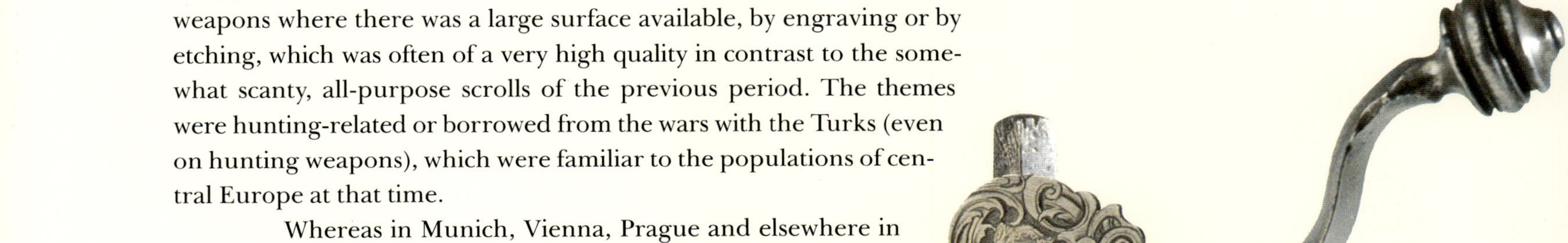

Lockplate with internal wheellock by Johann Georg Dax (Munich, c. 1730). Intaglio engraving of a wild boar hunt, surrounded by rococo ornamentation.

Museum of Weapons, Liège.

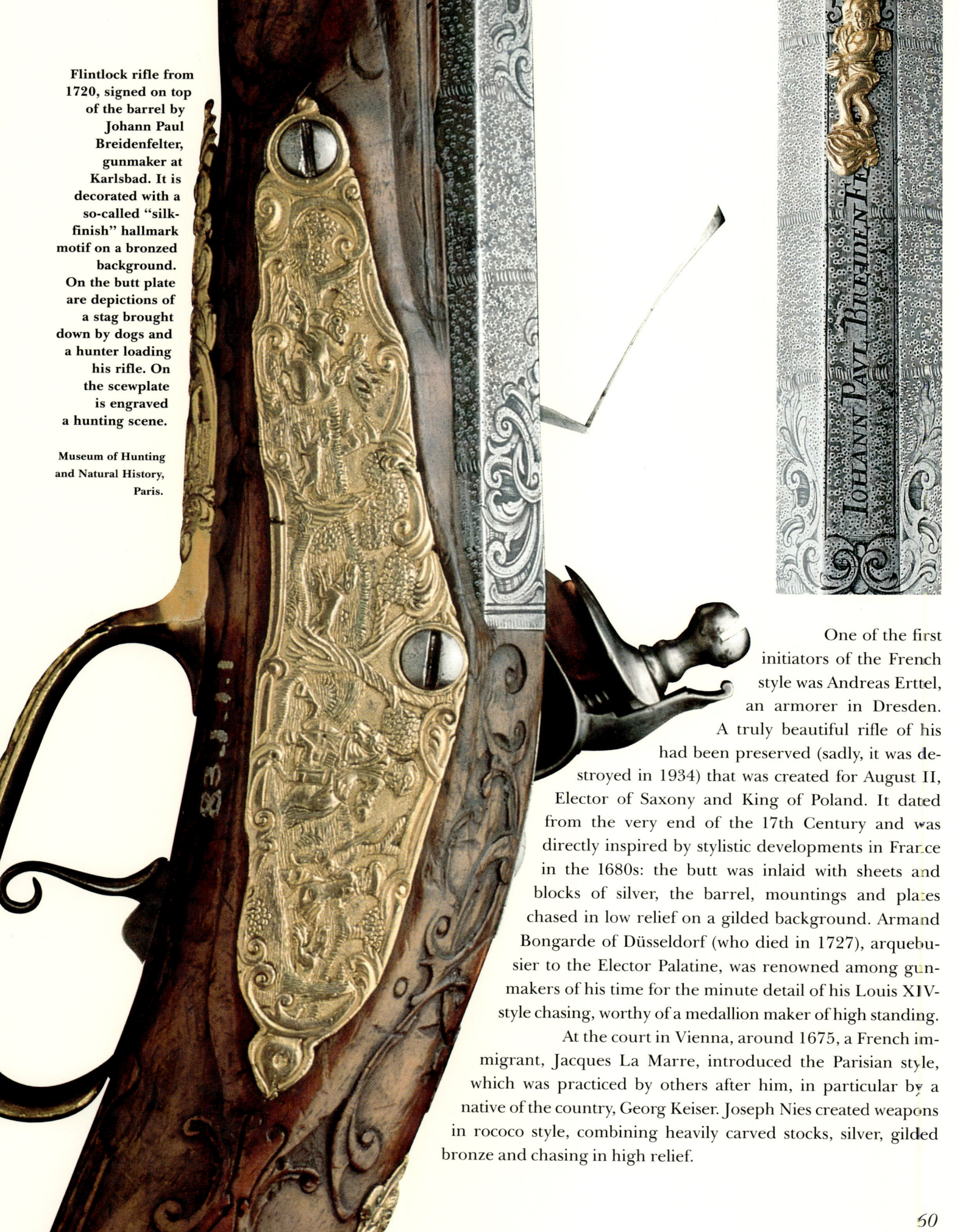

Flintlock rifle from 1720, signed on top of the barrel by Johann Paul Breidenfelter, gunmaker at Karlsbad. It is decorated with a so-called "silk-finish" hallmark motif on a bronzed background. On the butt plate are depictions of a stag brought down by dogs and a hunter loading his rifle. On the scewplate is engraved a hunting scene.

Museum of Hunting and Natural History, Paris.

One of the first initiators of the French style was Andreas Erttel, an armorer in Dresden. A truly beautiful rifle of his had been preserved (sadly, it was destroyed in 1934) that was created for August II, Elector of Saxony and King of Poland. It dated from the very end of the 17th Century and was directly inspired by stylistic developments in France in the 1680s: the butt was inlaid with sheets and blocks of silver, the barrel, mountings and plates chased in low relief on a gilded background. Armand Bongarde of Düsseldorf (who died in 1727), arquebusier to the Elector Palatine, was renowned among gunmakers of his time for the minute detail of his Louis XIV-style chasing, worthy of a medallion maker of high standing.

At the court in Vienna, around 1675, a French immigrant, Jacques La Marre, introduced the Parisian style, which was practiced by others after him, in particular by a native of the country, Georg Keiser. Joseph Nies created weapons in rococo style, combining heavily carved stocks, silver, gilded bronze and chasing in high relief.

Wheellock rifle adorned in brass engraved with stags and wild boars by Bartomoleus Daisenberger in Munich (mid-18th Century).

Museum of Hunting and Natural History, Paris

Detail of the rifle shown opposite. The cheekpiece is decorated with the coat of arms of its owner. Bartolomeus Daisenberger worked for the court of Bavaria between 1746 and 1777.

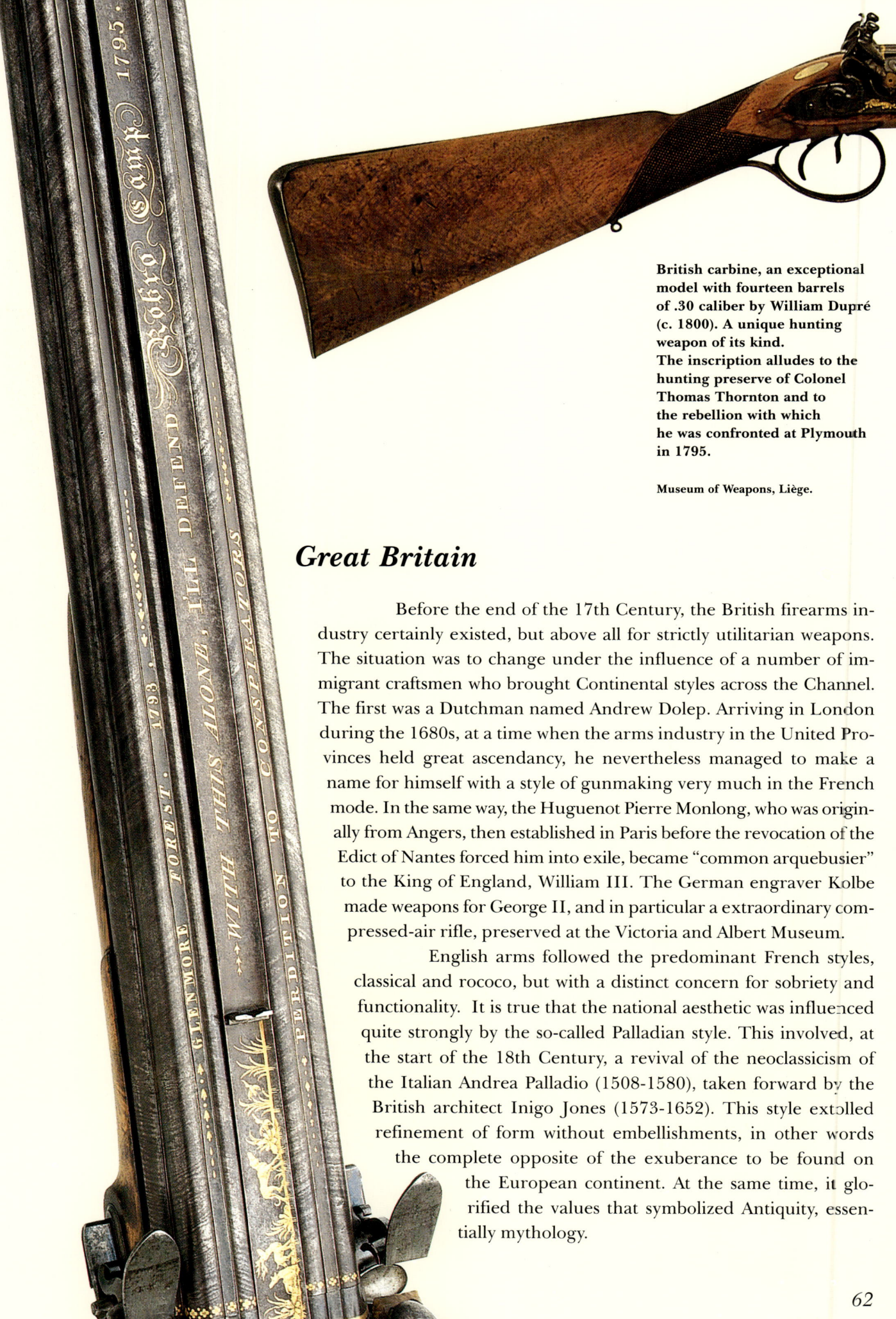

British carbine, an exceptional model with fourteen barrels of .30 caliber by William Dupré (c. 1800). A unique hunting weapon of its kind. The inscription alludes to the hunting preserve of Colonel Thomas Thornton and to the rebellion with which he was confronted at Plymouth in 1795.

Museum of Weapons, Liège.

Great Britain

Before the end of the 17th Century, the British firearms industry certainly existed, but above all for strictly utilitarian weapons. The situation was to change under the influence of a number of immigrant craftsmen who brought Continental styles across the Channel. The first was a Dutchman named Andrew Dolep. Arriving in London during the 1680s, at a time when the arms industry in the United Provinces held great ascendancy, he nevertheless managed to make a name for himself with a style of gunmaking very much in the French mode. In the same way, the Huguenot Pierre Monlong, who was originally from Angers, then established in Paris before the revocation of the Edict of Nantes forced him into exile, became "common arquebusier" to the King of England, William III. The German engraver Kolbe made weapons for George II, and in particular a extraordinary compressed-air rifle, preserved at the Victoria and Albert Museum.

English arms followed the predominant French styles, classical and rococo, but with a distinct concern for sobriety and functionality. It is true that the national aesthetic was influenced quite strongly by the so-called Palladian style. This involved, at the start of the 18th Century, a revival of the neoclassicism of the Italian Andrea Palladio (1508-1580), taken forward by the British architect Inigo Jones (1573-1652). This style extolled refinement of form without embellishments, in other words the complete opposite of the exuberance to be found on the European continent. At the same time, it glorified the values that symbolized Antiquity, essentially mythology.

Towards 1750, decorators of weapons introduced Chinese ornamentation, fashionable decorative motifs (mandarins, pagodas, exotic animals and plants), especially on the stocks.

About twenty years later, the neoclassical style supplanted all the others and remained in favor in England until the beginning of the 19th Century. It developed independently, compared to the neoclassical style in the rest of Europe, but as their themes were common they naturally had great similarities. The difference was that the British mode was less sumptuous, and could never rival the style of a Boutet, for example, even though the quality of English weapons around 1800 was just as high as that of other gunmaking countries.

Detail of the carbine shown above. It is accompanied by a magazine for loading powder into seven barrels at once. Furthermore it could could be transformed into two rifles of seven barrels, with the help of alternative mountings.

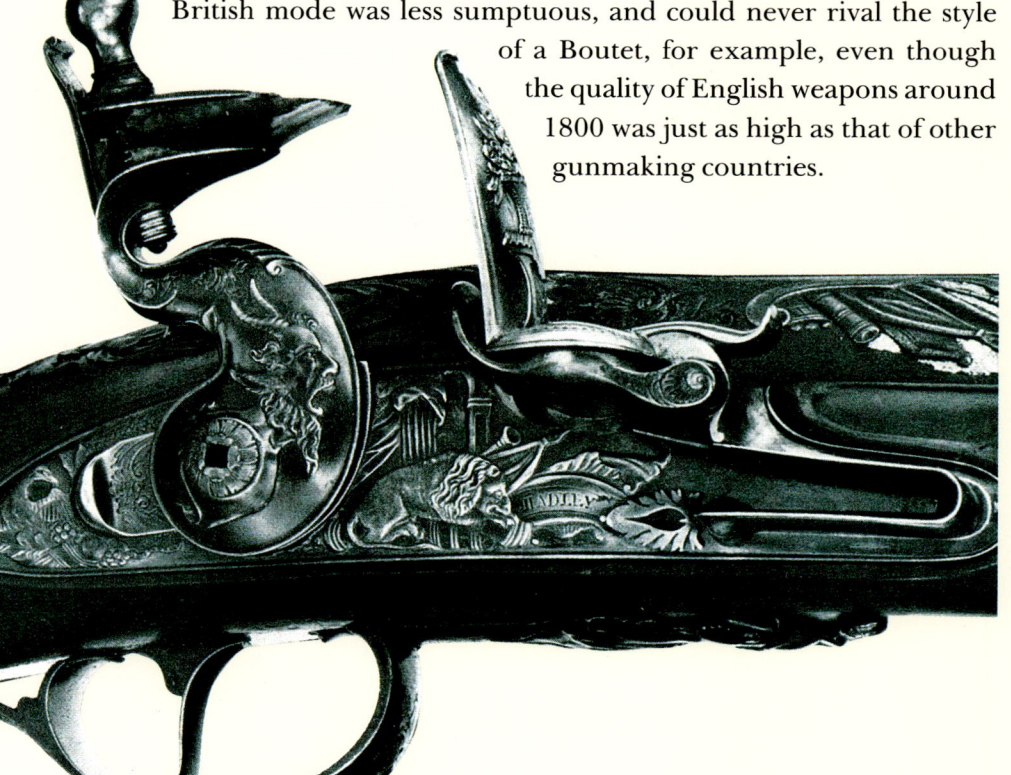

Detail of an English flintlock, chased and embellished with silver. Lockplate by Henry Hadley, barrel by Thomas Hudson, 1744-1745. The decoration depicts the British lion on a background of trophies. The hammer is decorated with the head of a satyr in low relief.

Royal collections at Windsor.

Hunting weapon from 1775, with fluted "Madrid style" butt: the work of Michele Battista, craftsman of the royal factory in Naples, who worked for the kings of the Two Sicilies.

Museum of Weapons, Liège.

Above and right. The powder flask in translucent horn is richly chased, inlaid and gilded.

Italy

Detail of the flintlock, where the combined elements—frizzen, pan, hammer, trigger and the sideplate, showing a hunter at rest, stroking his dog—present a decorative extravaganza with chasing and gilded inlay. The background is "water" blued.

During the second half of the 17th Century, the French influence was never absent from Italy, but the craftsmen of the Adriatic Peninsula developed a decorative style of their own, supported by a flourishing virtuosity. Brescia retained its pre-eminence in weapons manufacture and, for several

The blued barrel with damascene work is decorated in scrolls and anthropomorphic figures.

more decades, took pride of place over other regions of Italy in the production of luxury items. It was notable, however, that the preference for openwork iron appliqués, in lace style, gave way to deep chasing, in the round, of figures in animal and human form. At the same time, the buttstocks matched the taste of the day, with silver inlay and subsequently brass appliqués. However, the profusion and extreme richness of the chased high-reliefs could not hide the fact that these works were not the result of court art but reflected an inspiration and a rendering of details from a more popular and sometimes more clumsy origin.

Outside Brescia, talented decorators were found in many places, from the Bologna region to Rome. Assimilating the classical and rococo styles, these craftsmen integrated them into their local style, which was extremely florid and spectacular, generally favoring heavy chasing as opposed to low-relief and intaglio engraving. At the same time, they displayed significant conservatism in the forms and decorations inherited from the 17th Century, which lasted almost until 1800.

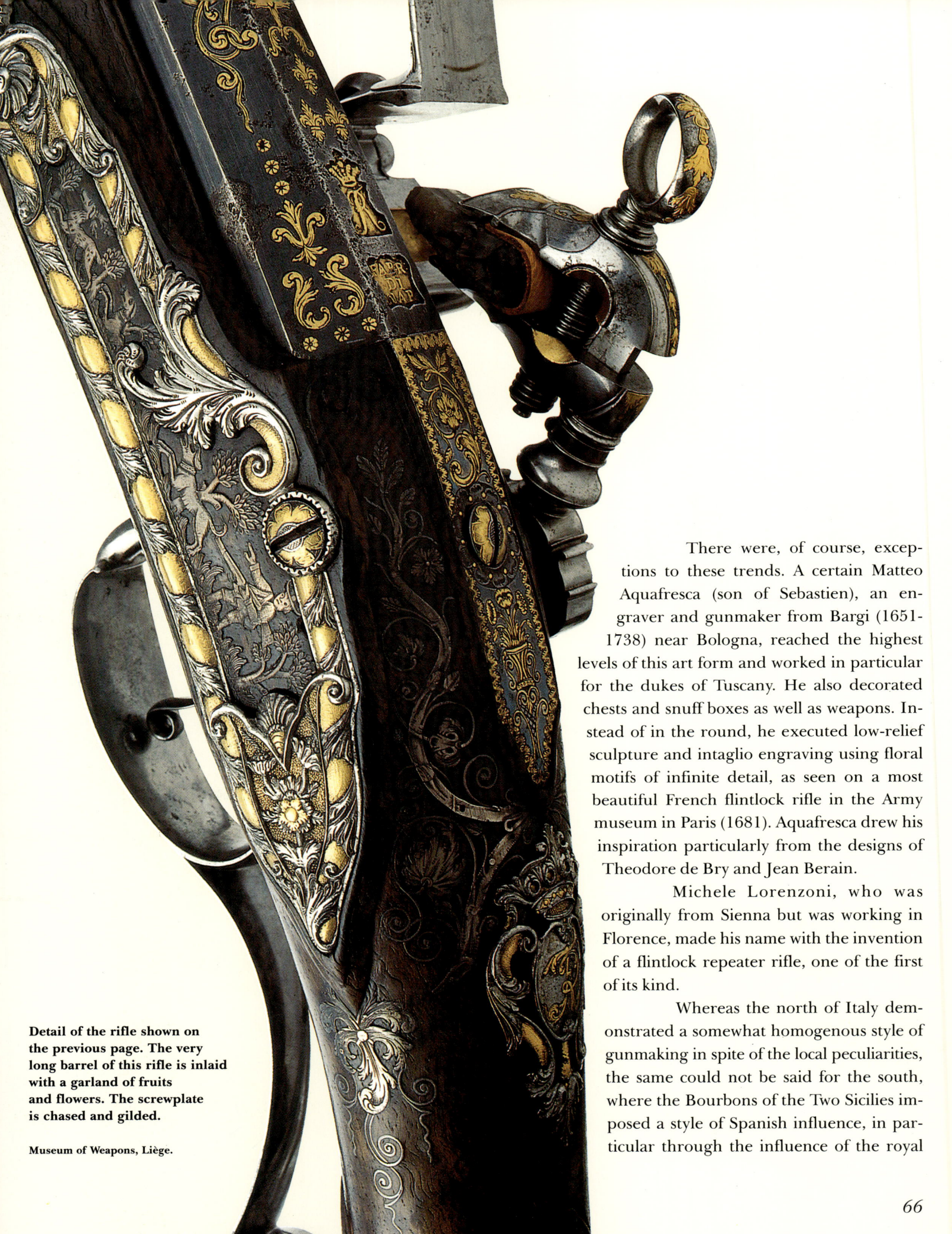

Detail of the rifle shown on the previous page. The very long barrel of this rifle is inlaid with a garland of fruits and flowers. The screwplate is chased and gilded.

Museum of Weapons, Liège.

There were, of course, exceptions to these trends. A certain Matteo Aquafresca (son of Sebastien), an engraver and gunmaker from Bargi (1651-1738) near Bologna, reached the highest levels of this art form and worked in particular for the dukes of Tuscany. He also decorated chests and snuff boxes as well as weapons. Instead of in the round, he executed low-relief sculpture and intaglio engraving using floral motifs of infinite detail, as seen on a most beautiful French flintlock rifle in the Army museum in Paris (1681). Aquafresca drew his inspiration particularly from the designs of Theodore de Bry and Jean Berain.

Michele Lorenzoni, who was originally from Sienna but was working in Florence, made his name with the invention of a flintlock repeater rifle, one of the first of its kind.

Whereas the north of Italy demonstrated a somewhat homogenous style of gunmaking in spite of the local peculiarities, the same could not be said for the south, where the Bourbons of the Two Sicilies imposed a style of Spanish influence, in particular through the influence of the royal

False lockplate chased by an anonymous master from Citto di Castello (Umbria, Italy). The chasing depicts the suicide of Anthony after the battle of Actium, framed by two allegorical figures. The decoration is inspired by the French collections of designs by Thuraine and Le Hollandois and François Marcou (18th Century).

Museum of Weapons, Liège

Flint rifle in wood, iron and gold by Michele Battista (Naples, 1770-1775). The detail reveals, engraved in a medallion, the bust of a knight wearing a helmet and the letter R with a crown above it, as a reminder that the rifle came from the royal Factory of Naples.

Museum of Hunting and Natural History, Paris.

factory in Naples, which they created in 1757. From the start of the century, the Neapolitan gunmakers had developed a specialty in tortoiseshell marquetry on butts.

The premier artisan of the royal factory of Naples was Michele Battista. He used an abundance of classical-style ornamentation, engraved, chased and damascened trophies and hunting scenes, as well as characters and scrolls inlaid in silver on the butts. This ornamental style was drawn both from the tradition inherited from the beginning of the century and from popular imagination. The rococo style no longer appeared. On the contrary, the French occupation of the Italian principalities brought to these regions the Empire style, which was to last in Italy into the first decades of the 19th Century.

Breechloading flintlock rifle by Lejeune at Liège (c. 1760). The engraving and carving are in the rococo style.

Museum of Weapons, Liège.

Screwplate of a rifle by Claude Niquet (Liège, c. 1730), once belonging to the Grand Duke of Saxe-Weimar. Gilded bronze. The motif is inspired by the Parisian designs of Lacollombe.

Museum of Weapons, Liège.

The Netherlands and Liège

In the 17th Century, the United Provinces (the area that is now the Netherlands) and the principality of Liège rose to the rank of top weapons producer in Europe. They did not, however, enter the luxury weapons market. Placing greater importance on military equipment and utilitarian equipment for hunting and defense, they began to export these types of products throughout the world. With the exception of the pistols from Maastricht with ivory stocks dating from 1650-1660, of great originality and high quality, one has to wait until the end of the century to see fine weapons from these regions emerging outside their country of origin. Utrecht, Maastricht and Amsterdam, principally, as well as Liège, which eventually overtook them, were the home of an important arms trade in which many well-known gunmakers flourished: Cornelis Coster, Lasonder, the Pentermans, Louroux, Beckers, De La Pierre, Behr, Thiermay, Devillers, Massin, the Niquets and others.

Their decorative style followed the French mode with the peculiarity that they remained faithful to them for longer than did Paris: the decorators in the reign of Louis XIV predominated until the 1740s and the rococo genre lasted on into the 1770s; only the Louis XVI style was cut short, "wiped out" by the Revolution since it found itself between a Louis XV and an Empire style imposed on it in its hour of glory. Compared to the French style, guns of the Low

Gentleman returning from the hunt holding a classic hunting rifle with a so-called "ham" butt. Detail of a painting by Hendrick van der Neer Eglon (1634-1703).

Museum of Fine Arts, Lille

Countries were somewhat "provincial," less sumptuous and sometimes less delicate, and showed more abundant use of carved fittings in iron or cast and gilded brass. Several manufacturers from Liège added the words "in Paris" to their signature in order to increase the value of their products. The Dutchman Wernand Droogbrood translated his name as PAYN CEC (*"pain sec"* or dry bread), following the example of those in the Germanic countries who prided themselves on understanding the language of Racine and Voltaire.

Although the weapons industry began to decline in the United Provinces in the 18th Century, that of Liège grew considerably. Chasers, copper casters and gilders provided custom work for the gunmakers, who subcontracted various operations of weapons manufacture to people working at home. The degree of luxury of these products depended on the fortune of the clients who were mostly lesser nobility or the local or foreign bourgeoisie; the absence of royal commissions prevented these craftsmen from working to the best of their ability, unlike their colleagues in the large capitals. The political union with France, between 1794 and 1814, was profitable for the better of them as it put the finishing touches on their training and familiarized them with the demands of a large state. Furthermore, it is interesting to see the neo-classical work of a certain Jean-Toussaint Renkin, on an outstanding rifle presented to the First Consul by the weapons manufacturers of Liège in 1803 (Paris, museum of Hunting and Nature), and certain works of Devillers, Biron and Berleur. Throughout these works, it is very clear that, in the applied arts more than anywhere, it was the opportunities for work that created the talent.

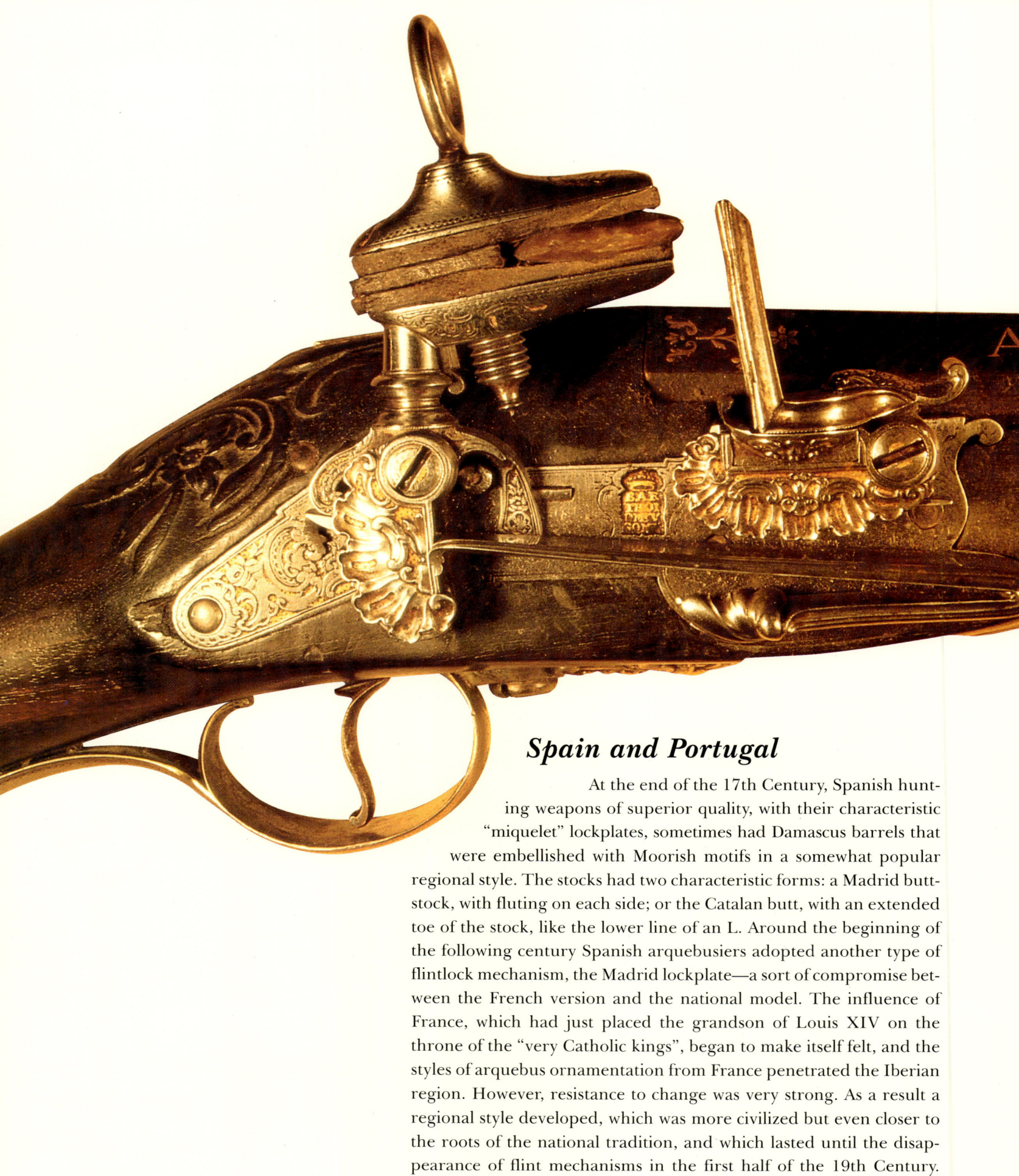

Spain and Portugal

At the end of the 17th Century, Spanish hunting weapons of superior quality, with their characteristic "miquelet" lockplates, sometimes had Damascus barrels that were embellished with Moorish motifs in a somewhat popular regional style. The stocks had two characteristic forms: a Madrid buttstock, with fluting on each side; or the Catalan butt, with an extended toe of the stock, like the lower line of an L. Around the beginning of the following century Spanish arquebusiers adopted another type of flintlock mechanism, the Madrid lockplate—a sort of compromise between the French version and the national model. The influence of France, which had just placed the grandson of Louis XIV on the throne of the "very Catholic kings", began to make itself felt, and the styles of arquebus ornamentation from France penetrated the Iberian region. However, resistance to change was very strong. As a result a regional style developed, which was more civilized but even closer to the roots of the national tradition, and which lasted until the disappearance of flint mechanisms in the first half of the 19th Century.

Detail of a flintlock rifle made by Bartholomeu Gomes, head of the arsenal in Lisbon, between 1722 and 1776. The miquelet lockplate, chased with rococo motifs and inlaid with gold, bears the stamp of the gunsmaker and the date, 1772. The barrel, dating from 1776, is by the same artist. This rifle belonged to the famous Marquis of Pombal, prime minister to King Joseph I.

Rainer Daehnhardt collection, Portugal.

Imagine a typical Spanish hunting rifle of this period: it was fitted with a single barrel (of European manufacture, moreover), embellished on the breech in gold damascene work with the name and stamp of the gunmaker and the barrel-maker. The lockplate was generally of blued steel, accented with delicate chasing and inlay. The stock was of fruitwood, which was sometimes stained, or more rarely in walnut with usually a Madrid or French butt, possibly inlaid with silver motifs. Mountings of chased steel were most common. The ornamental style incorporated classical elements, a subdued rococo style and, at the end of the 18th Century, neoclassical motifs. In contrast, the Boutet style, which could be associated with the Napoleonic invaders, was categorically thrown out for nationalist reasons. In Spain, production of weaponry was concentrated in Madrid, in Ripoll in Catalonia, and in Eibar in the Basque country.

Portuguese hunting weapons in the 18th Century and the beginning of the 19th, although very well known, did not differ fundamentally from Spanish. The fluted butt, the damascus barrel, the chased and inlaid lockplate, the iron or sometimes silver mountings that were engraved and inlaid, all testified to a common inspiration, sustained by the grand styles of the period but embellished to local tastes. Numerous workshops in both the capital and the provinces contributed to this production, but the kings of Portugal raised the level of quality even higher by ordering the manufacture of luxury weapons at the arsenal in Lisbon, where they brought together the best craftsmen.

Detail of the rifle shown below. The bronze appliqué on the right side of the buttstock depicts a Turkish archer.

Hermitage Museum, St.Petersburg.

Russia

Left side of a Russian flintlock rifle (Toula, 1740-1750). The screwplate is of silver, the block inlaid in the butt is of bronze damascene work.

Hermitage Museum, St.Petersburg.

Russia continued to open up to the Western world throughout the 17th Century. But the production from the arsenal in the Kremlin retained its regional and traditional character in spite of certain influences, gleaned here and there, from foreign gunmakers. The buttstocks had inlaid ornaments that evoked oriental motifs and the chasing on the metal areas mixed European ornamentation with that derived from popular Russian art.

In 1705, Tsar Peter the Great, obsessed by the westernisation of his country, established a factory for hand-held weapons at Toula, south of Moscow, which would also make luxury weapons for use by the sovereign and the court, or intended as diplomatic gifts. This enterprise employed many master gunmakers recruited from abroad, mostly from Germany and Scandinavia, and some craftsmen executed custom work at home. Echoes of popu-

Left side of a flintlock musket once belonging to Frederick I of Sweden. The screwplate is chased in the international rococo style widespread in Europe in the middle of the 18th Century, due in particular to the mobility of certain craftsmen.

Museum of Weapons, Liège.

lar local art were common in the production of luxury weapons from Toula. However, it was the eastern style that nevertheless predominated, with a French influence on the ornamentation that came from the collections of designs and above all from immigrant craftsmen, who were steeped in the Parisian mode. The belated Louis XIV style, rococo and neoclassicism are noticeable in these weapons, but sometimes mixed together.

Chasing played an important role. It covered the barrels with laceworks of arabesques and garlands surrounding the images. The plates had the same finish, with subjects and hunting scenes in low relief. The backgrounds were often gilded, in certain cases with inlay, with mountings sometimes in gilded bronze. The stocks were adorned with thin lines and motifs in silver or, more rarely, simply carved. The most beautiful weapons were made in the reign of the Empress Elizabeth Petranova, in the middle of the 18th Century. Towards the end of the century, however, there was a decline in quality. The chasing was replaced by inlay of various metals, precious and otherwise, giving these guns a somewhat gaudy appearance. This became a sort of resurgence of ancestral craftsmanship, based on the local style of embellishment of metals. Outside Toula, St.Petersburg also made a name for itself as a producer of luxury weapons.

America

Since they were of neither social nor practical value in a land of pioneers, there were few luxury weapons in use in the colonies of North America in this period. Those few which were there (before the beginning of the 20th Century) came from the Old World, and were made by British or French gunmakers. However, around 1750, in the English colonies of Pennsylvania and Maryland (and later also in Virginia and North Carolina), a type of weapon was developed, with a

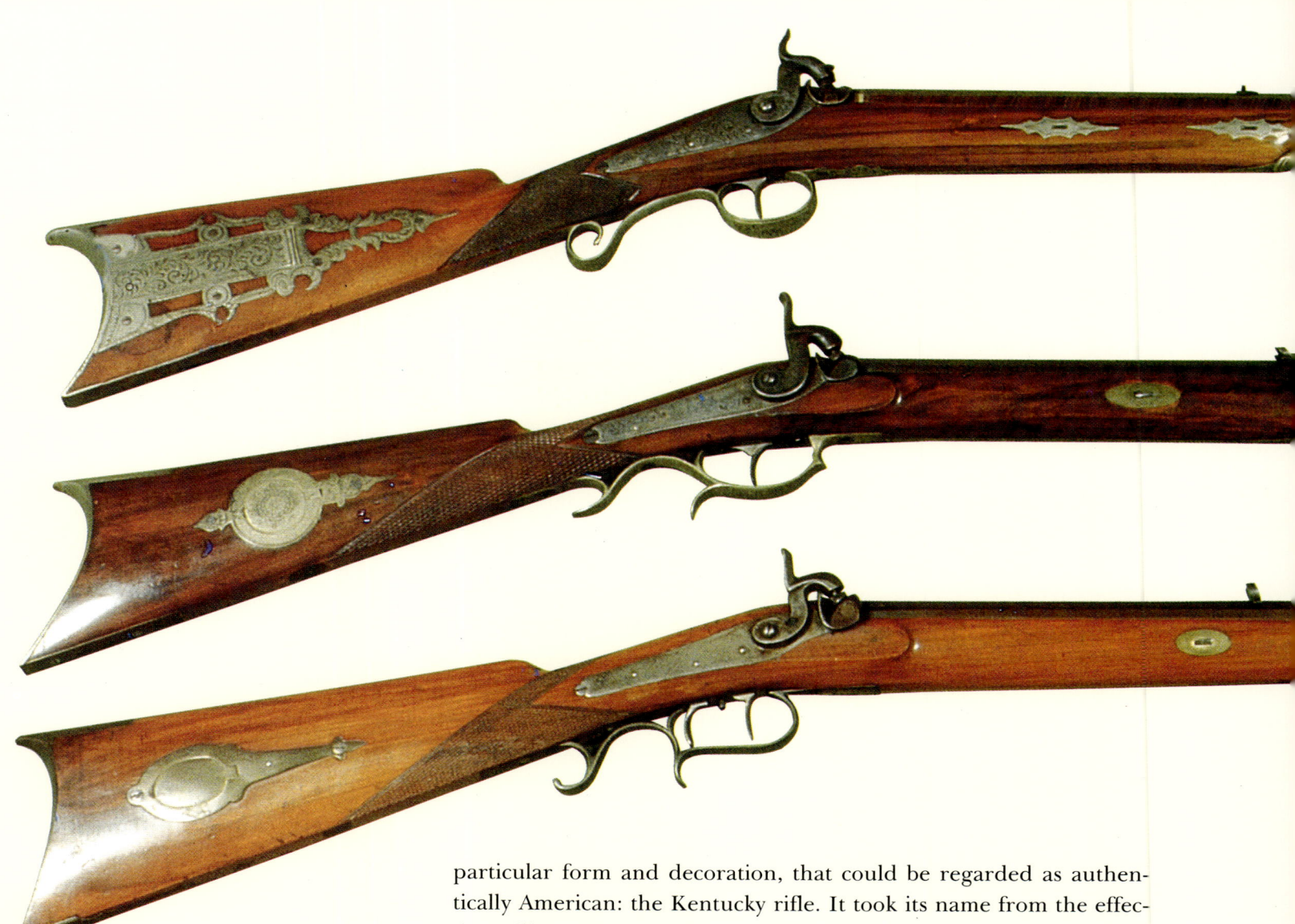

particular form and decoration, that could be regarded as authentically American: the Kentucky rifle. It took its name from the effective military use made of it in 1814, by a corps of volunteers from this territory, but it was in fact made by craftsmen in the Pennsylvania region. The Kentucky rifle was derived from German rifled weapons, brought to America or made there by immigrants. This model was adapted to the local conditions and became the typical American model in the mid-18th Century. It continued to evolve until its disappearance around 1850.

The weapon was characterized by its great length, 54 to 64 inches, and by its bore, which was relatively small for the period, .32 to .60 caliber. It had a long stock of maple, with a small, sloping comb. The flintlock, and later the percussion lock, was almost always bare of decoration; this was applied instead to the stock. Early Kentucky rifles had German-style bullet boxes housed in the buttstocks with sliding covers. The butt itself was sparsely carved with some moldings.

During the last quarter of the century, the Kentucky rifle acquired its classic configuration. The bullet box lost its sliding cover in favor of a hinged lid, and was framed by a brass mounting of spectacular dimensions, shaped and sparsely engraved. The cheekpiece was inlaid in brass and often finished off with a C-shaped heelplate—or, more rarely, a representation of a figure. Sometimes this carving was

replaced by a second brass inlay. The other parts of the stock, in particular the hand guard, also acquired some inlaid subject. The metal was brass, sometimes nickel silver or, more rarely, silver, in later examples built as presentation weapons.

Whether carving or inlay, the decorative elements originated from two sources: first, elements borrowed from the European rococo style; and second, a throng of motifs and subjects related to popular art and thought, whose profound significance was undoubtedly often not noticed by those who created them. As result one finds many religious or talismanic symbols such as the monogram of Christ or the fish, the heart symbolizing the fifth wound of Christ, the eight-pointed star of Bethlehem, the dove, the three-petalled tulip of the Trinity, the crescent moon evoking the Virgin, and various astrological motifs. One also comes across a number of representations of familiar animals, anthropomorphic heads and interwoven vegetation, as well as the American eagle, the supreme patriotic emblem of the United States.

Although in ornamentation Kentucky rifles could not be compared with the luxury weapons produced in Europe at the same time, they constituted a no less original approach, in their unique environment, to embellishing a utilitarian object despite the limited means available.

**Kentucky-type rifles with percussion locks, made in Liège around 1840, probably for the United States.
The mountings in nickel silver are inspired by American designs but are engraved in European taste.
The most remarkable elements are the covers of the bullet boxes in the buttstocks.**

Museum of Weapons, Liège.

THE 19TH CENTURY

Detail of a double-gun by Antoine Rongé Brothers (1844, Liège).
The hammers are chased in the shape of a dolphin, an ornamentation
typical of the 19th Century.

Museum of Weapons, Liège.

Double shotgun rifle for pinfire cartridges, Lefaucheux system, 16 bore (1865). This is a perfect illustration of the combination of several styles from across Europe in the creation of a weapon of high quality. A mix of Renaissance style and the realist genre of the 19th Century.

Museum of Weapons, Liège.

The 19th Century, in terms of decorative arts, was characterized by a total incapacity to create an original style of its own, if one ignores the Art Nouveau of the latter years. However, its goldsmiths, engravers and sculptors equaled, if not surpassed, those who had preceded them. But their creativity lay in the combination of known elements, reinterpreted in their own fashion. It was the great period of the "neo" styles: neoceltic, neoroman, neogothic, neo-Renaissance, neo-Louis XIV, neo-Louis XVI...

Luxury weapons were strongly influenced by these fashions, incorporating them sometimes, or more often only retaining certain significant elements and limiting their imitation to varying degrees. This trend, which was called eclecticism because it preferred to select from prior experience rather than to innovate, was accompanied by a "horror of emptiness". Ornamentation even supplanted utility, in particular on weapons for exhibition or display whose goal was to offer a medium—if not a pretext—for exuberant and ostentatious decoration. Arms produced for competitions, national exhibitions and (from 1851 onwards) World Expositions, or as presents intended for heads of state, were most representative of the tastes, techniques and extravagances of this time. Alongside this, luxury weapons that tried to be functional also reflected contemporary artistic customs and talents but with less brilliance.

Here again, some "large-scale" works emerged from among the most highly rated artisans. It was to them that the most beautiful

Details of the hammer, the trigger guard and the triggers of the gun shown on the right. The damascus barrels are by Bernard (Paris). The chasing and the rich damascene gold work are attributed to Joseph Boussart of Liège.

Detail of the gun shown on the left. Under the trigger guard can be seen some magnificent chasing, depicting a dog flushing a pair of partridges.

Double-barrel percussion shotgun rifle by Haaken-Plomdeur, of Liège, in 14 bore. The English stock is delicately carved in the so-called Louis XIV style. Also of note is the rich gold inlay—in relief on a gray engraved background—embellishing the lockplates, breeches and mountings, by J.J.Cloes. The stock is of carved walnut.

Museum of Weapons, Liège.

Detail of the gun shown above. In front of the trigger guard, the walnut stock is carved with animal motifs.

pieces were entrusted and, as under the Ancien Régime, often several of them would get together to decorate these special arms. And whereas the name of the gunmaker who entrusted the artistic work to them was almost always known, theirs did not necessarily appear in the signatures and hallmarks. In such cases, archive documents can help to identify them. In exceptional circumstances, an additional decorator was called in to design the overall composition, the harmonious organization of the various decorative elements on the weapon. As in earlier centuries, the people who practiced these artistic professions did not necessarily limit themselves to weaponry. They could also be found in various other fields: goldsmithing, jewelry, furniture, artistic casting, etc.

As for those who decorated the more ordinary weapons, they were often condemned to anonymity. This was often so for stockmakers and more modest engravers, who were subcontractors to the gunmakers and worked behind the scenes at the mercy of the markets. Or they were simply employees of master craftsmen who were prosperous and highly respected. Only those weapons intended for well-off clients were entrusted to reputed decorators whose identity, although rarely revealed by a signature, was nevertheless known by word of mouth. It was only in the 20th Century that the custom spread, although not

Detail of the gun shown above. The five-ribbed damascus barrels were executed by Bernard.

widely, of having the name of the engraver as well as the maker appear on luxury weapons. This initiative was more the result of a desire to foil forgeries than of any concern for the artist.

The stockmakers of the 19th Century opted increasingly for walnut, which then became the material of choice for the manufacture of stocks. All the same, for display weapons other materials were often used, such as ebony, rosewood, mahogany or even ivory.

The principal centers of the luxury arms industry at this time were Paris, Liège and London, each contributing in a very different way to the development of hunting weapons. Paris benefited from the contributions of the whole of France, in particular Saint-Etienne. Until around 1860, Paris innovated in technical matters and it dominated Europe in terms of luxury articles, including weapons. It worked in close collaboration with Liège—which became the top military and civilian weapons producer in the world around 1900—partly through subcontracting work and partly because since the Middle Ages, through its combination of language and thought, Paris had exercised a strong attraction for artists and craftsmen from Liège. Towards the end of the century, when, with passing fashions, Paris no longer set the tone in weaponry, Liège took over the lead in the field of ornamentation.

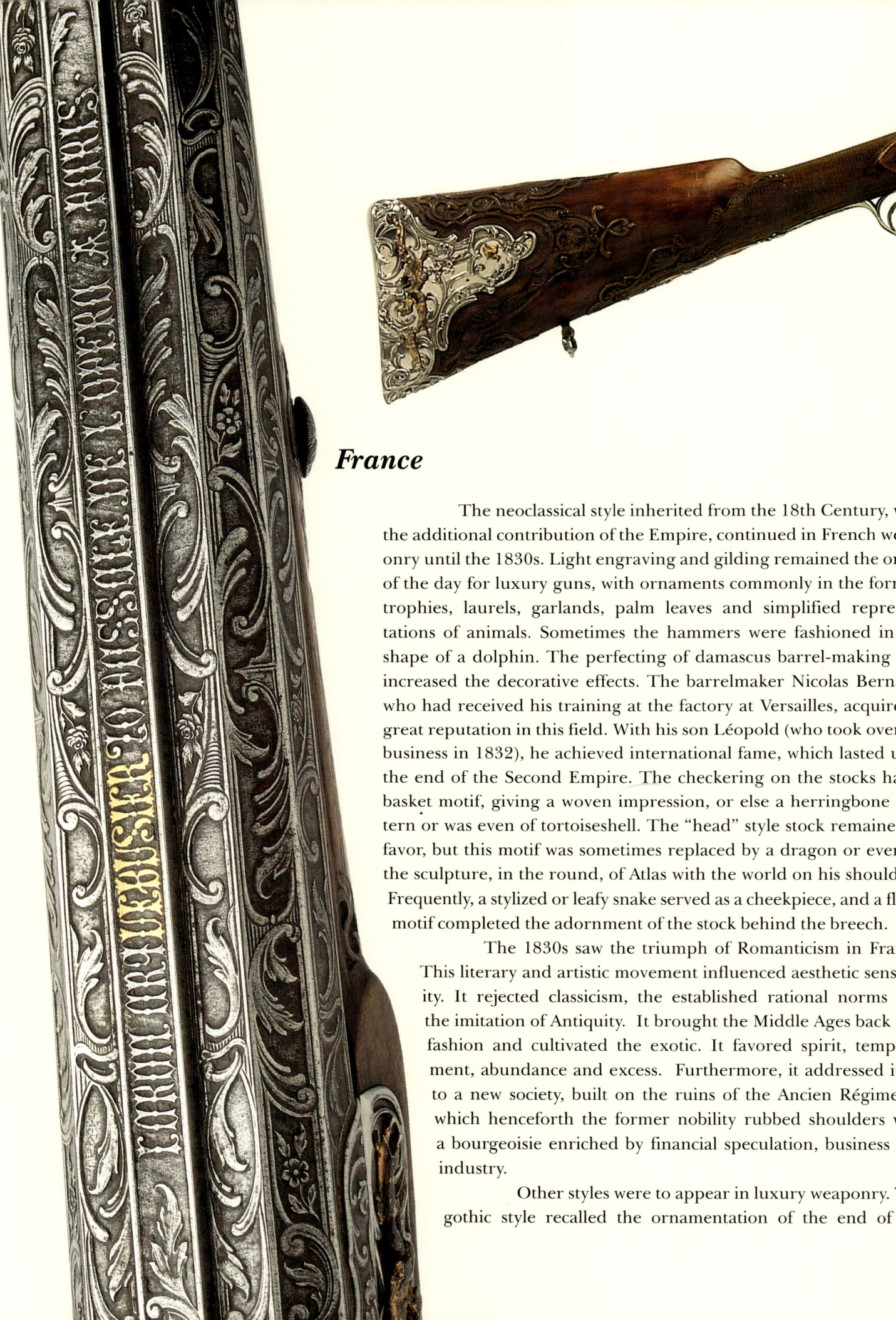

France

The neoclassical style inherited from the 18th Century, with the additional contribution of the Empire, continued in French weaponry until the 1830s. Light engraving and gilding remained the order of the day for luxury guns, with ornaments commonly in the form of trophies, laurels, garlands, palm leaves and simplified representations of animals. Sometimes the hammers were fashioned in the shape of a dolphin. The perfecting of damascus barrel-making also increased the decorative effects. The barrelmaker Nicolas Bernard, who had received his training at the factory at Versailles, acquired a great reputation in this field. With his son Léopold (who took over his business in 1832), he achieved international fame, which lasted until the end of the Second Empire. The checkering on the stocks had a basket motif, giving a woven impression, or else a herringbone pattern or was even of tortoiseshell. The "head" style stock remained in favor, but this motif was sometimes replaced by a dragon or even by the sculpture, in the round, of Atlas with the world on his shoulders. Frequently, a stylized or leafy snake served as a cheekpiece, and a floral motif completed the adornment of the stock behind the breech.

The 1830s saw the triumph of Romanticism in France. This literary and artistic movement influenced aesthetic sensitivity. It rejected classicism, the established rational norms and the imitation of Antiquity. It brought the Middle Ages back into fashion and cultivated the exotic. It favored spirit, temperament, abundance and excess. Furthermore, it addressed itself to a new society, built on the ruins of the Ancien Régime, in which henceforth the former nobility rubbed shoulders with a bourgeoisie enriched by financial speculation, business and industry.

Other styles were to appear in luxury weaponry. The gothic style recalled the ornamentation of the end of the

Double-barrelled gun c. 1840 signed on the finely worked barrels "Caron, arquebusier, 20, passage de l'Opéra, à Paris". This gun belonged to King Louis-Philippe.

Museum of Hunting and Natural History, Paris.
Loan from the Army museum.

The hammer is sculpted in the form of a dolphin with an angel riding it, holding a young wild boar in his hands. The trigger guard is embellished with a lion's head and the sideplate depicts dogs with a kill. The gilding has disappeared on most of the chasing.

Above: detail of a double-barrel Lefaucheux-system 12-bore gun. The damascus barrel were executed by Léopold Bernard, in Paris.

Museum of Weapons, Liège.

Middle Ages: octagonal or round barrels, decorated with longitudinal ribs and ending in lancets or trefoils, recesses and fenestration, or indeed with figurines and gargoyles added on top. Sometimes, this "cathedral" style was made more complex by using characters in 15th or 16th Century costume to give a so-called "troubadour" theatrical effect. The neo-Renaissance style borrowed its motifs from the late Renaissance: scrolls, chimeras and devilry, "animal hides" and acanthus leaves. The neo-Louis XIV collapsed under the weight of its heavy scallops, as the so-called "Pompadour" neo-rococo did under the Louis XV rocaille, although with a certain amount of delicacy. In contrast, the "Marie-Antoinette" genre was inspired by the end-of-century ribbons and flowers. The Moorish style, as its name suggests, used geometric motifs, arabesques and features of Arab architecture, generally in outline.

Whatever the genre used, it was accompanied by ornamentation of vegetation, either in "fantasy" style, that is with a composition of abstract motifs derived from the natural world, or in "realistic" style —very much in fashion in the world of display weapons—which consisted of reproducing exactly the entanglement of roots, trunks or climbing plants. Hunting scenes were common, considering the intended use of the weapons decorated in this way.

Finally, the techniques used were aimed at creating effects. Chasing reigned on metal, creating subjects and ornaments sculpted in the round by carving away the support in openwork, or else intaglio engraving and inlay, flush or in relief. On the wooden parts relief sculpture was applied and gilded, and sometimes ivory, brass or silver were used.

The chasing on this double gun, in "fantasy vegetation" style, is superb. The inlay is in gold and the sculpture is of hunting motifs. This work of art, appeared at the World Exposition in Paris in 1855.

Museum of Weapons, Liège.

For utilitarian weapons, it was sufficient to have polished stocks with checkered grips, with intaglio and copperplate engraving. For presentation items, the themes and ornamental styles were often mixed together on a single weapon. On others of less exceptional quality, the historical reference was limited to one detail, or one or other motif, for example ribs carved on the barrels, or fancy hammers that evoked facets of gothic architecture.

The break with neoclassicism evidently appeared during the Exposition of industrial products in Paris, in 1835, where worthy of note were a gun exhibited by Alfred Gauvain, whose stock, carved or pierced by Liénard, featured in the round a hunter in Middle Age costume; another by Gernand Claudin, that was the work of six artists; a Renaissance-style rifle, Arab pistols, and "gothic" pistols illustrating scenes from the Crusades. Alphonse Caron, arquebusier to the king, exhibited a sword whose guard was a branch "carrying entwined along its length a snake, whose eyes are wide open at the sight of an 1100 franc diamond which sparkles on top of the shroud."

In 1836, the same Caron created a percussion gun in a chest, decorated with two-tone gold inlay of stylized vegetation and game fowl, the buttstock of which was of rhinoceros horn!

At the Exposition of French Industry of 1844, Devisme offered for display a double-barrel percussion gun, which is now to be found at Windsor Castle; it was acquired by King Louis-Philippe (whose monogram it bears) to be presented the following year to Prince Albert, husband of Queen Victoria. At the same time, Louis-Philippe had bought from Caron—intended for the same destination—another weapon with decoration entirely of hunting themes (now in the royal collection at Sandringham). For the world Exposition in London in 1851,

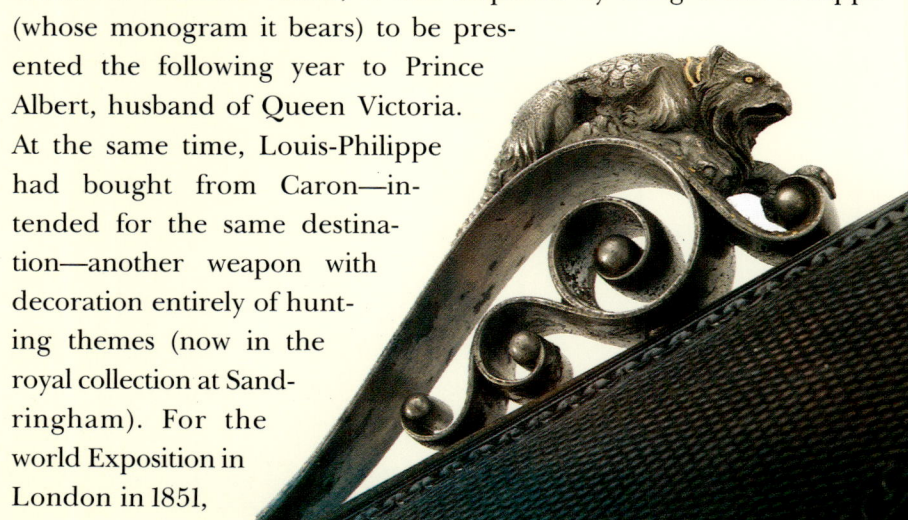

Percussion gun by Ronchard and Cizeron of Saint-Etienne. This gun, made for the World Exposition in Paris in 1900, won a gold medal there.

Museum of Hunting and Natural History, Paris. On loan from the Army museum.

86

Detail of the gun shown left. This splendid weapon is chased in early style in the grand tradition of Napoleon III, with dragons, lizards and snakes.

the first of its kind, LePage-Moutier exhibited a gun totally decorated in vegetation style. At the time of the second World Exposition, which was held in the French capital in 1855, the Parisian arquebusier André Fils presented a Lefaucheux rifle (Liège, Army museum) that was very richly chased with vine branches and had an ornate butt, in deep relief, with beautiful animal sculptures.

The world Exposition of 1867, in Paris, was the last of the Second Empire. Overdecorated weapons still held sway there, as well as the grandiose genre typical of the Napoleon III style.

The latter years saw the gradual disappearance of "sumptuous weapons" in favor of more refined models. The romantic genre had gone out of fashion. However, one could still find, at the world Exposition of 1900 in Paris, a percussion gun, chased in the early style with dragons, lizards and snakes, by Ronchard and Cizeron of Saint-Etienne. Moreover, it was this gun that won the gold medal.

Opposite and above: double barrel percussion shotgun by Mathieu Raick (Liège, 1828), 16 bore. The grip is executed in fine checkering and the butt is in "duck bill" style.

Museum of Weapons, Liège.

Liège

Incorporated into the double Kingdom of the Netherlands and Belgium after the fall of Napoleon, Liège had been part of the Belgian State since 1830. In this great center of weapons manufacture, the production of luxury weapons underwent a development very close to that in France, as much through the styles that were used as through diffusion of the "artistic professions" between Paris and this industrial town, some 230 miles away.

Here, the first Empire style in weaponry was to last until around 1840. Certain masterpieces of arquebus-making, preserved until today, testify to this fact, such as the beautiful weapon made by Mathieu Raick in 1828 (Museum of Weapons, Liège) or the set of guns and pistols executed by Joseph Devillers for the Prince of Orange the following year (Museum of Weapons, Liège).

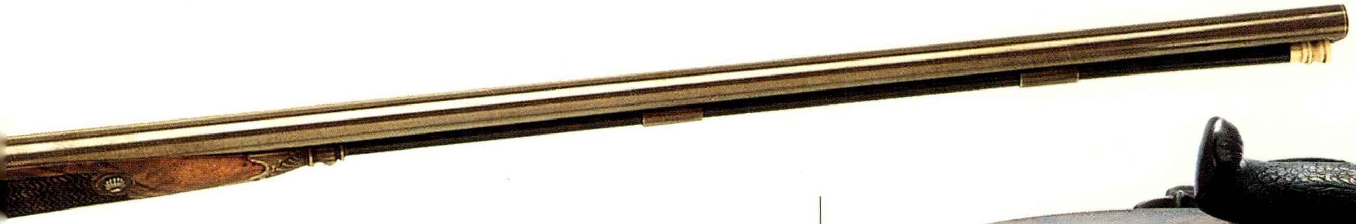

Detail of the gun shown left. The adornment is marbled and inlaid with gold. The damascus barrels are also inlaid.

Museum of Weapons, Liège.

Fitted case with 16-bore double percussion gun, made by Joseph Devillers (Liège, 1829) for the Prince of Orange. Barrels, sideplates and mountings are in fine damascene work, engraved and inlaid with gold. The coats of arms of the family of Orange are on the barrel beeches. The stock, in burl walnut, is delicately carved.

Museum of Weapons, Liège.

Above: engraving designs from a Lefaucheux gun by Joseph Boussart. Taken from the *Collection of ornaments* by Charles Claesen (1856).

Museum of Weapons, Liège.

It was during the 1840s that the Romantic tidal wave swept through the arquebus industry.

From 1856 onwards, the editor Charles Claesen published, in Liège, in several issues and in the form of separate plates, *a Collection of ornaments and subjects to be applied to the ornamentation of weapons taken from the designs of the principal artists*. Each of these plates depicted a shotgun, a pistol, a rifle, or a work in progress or executed by a decorator during recent years. Most of the works were Belgian, in this case from Liège, but some were French (Liénard and Rambert in Paris), Spanish (Placido Zuloaga) or Czech (Antoine and Ferdinand Lebeda in Prague). Moreover, the work was distributed in Paris, Leipzig and Berlin. In 1866, the same Claesen published again, in Liège and in Leipzig, another album of designs relating to industrial art in general, whose author was Liénard: *Specimens of decoration and ornamentation in the XIXth Century*. In the collection of 1856, ten decorators were featured: Joseph Boussart, Joseph Falloise, Charles Honoré, Nicolas Julin, Jean Herman, Joseph

"Burial of the hunter". Etching project for a plate executed by Lebeda Brothers in Prague. Taken from the *Collection of ornaments* by Charles Claesen (1856).

Museum of Weapons, Liège.

Neo-Renaissance ornament after Liénard. *Specimens for decoration and ornamentation in the XIXth century.* (Liège-Leipzig, 1866)

Museum of Weapons, Liège.

Waroux, J.J. Cloes, Lambert Donnay, Jean-Joseph Danse and Jean-Michel Tinlot. The latter was known as one of the best carvers of weapons of the century. Honoré and Julin had served their apprenticeships in Paris before becoming teachers of chasing at the Academy of Fine Arts in Liège. Boussart and Waroux were engravers and, in their youth, had attended this establishment, where the latter ended his career as a teacher. Like his father, Jean Herman was also there as a teacher of sculpture and ornament composition. Joseph Falloise and his son Louis were chasers. Danse and Donay also passed through the Academy and Danse taught the art of medals there. Other names were known as well, such as the engravers Charles Collinet and Léon Lemaître, or the chasers Potgisser and Cuvelier. Nearly all of them left behind works that can be found either in the museum of Weapons in Liège or in private collections, and which testify to their talent. Several had the opportunity to participate in the great world expositions and their names

Opposite and left page: designs for plates engraved with "vine leaf" ornaments and subjects by Joseph Falloise, taken from the *Collection of ornaments* by Charles Claesen (1856).

Museum of Weapons, Liège.

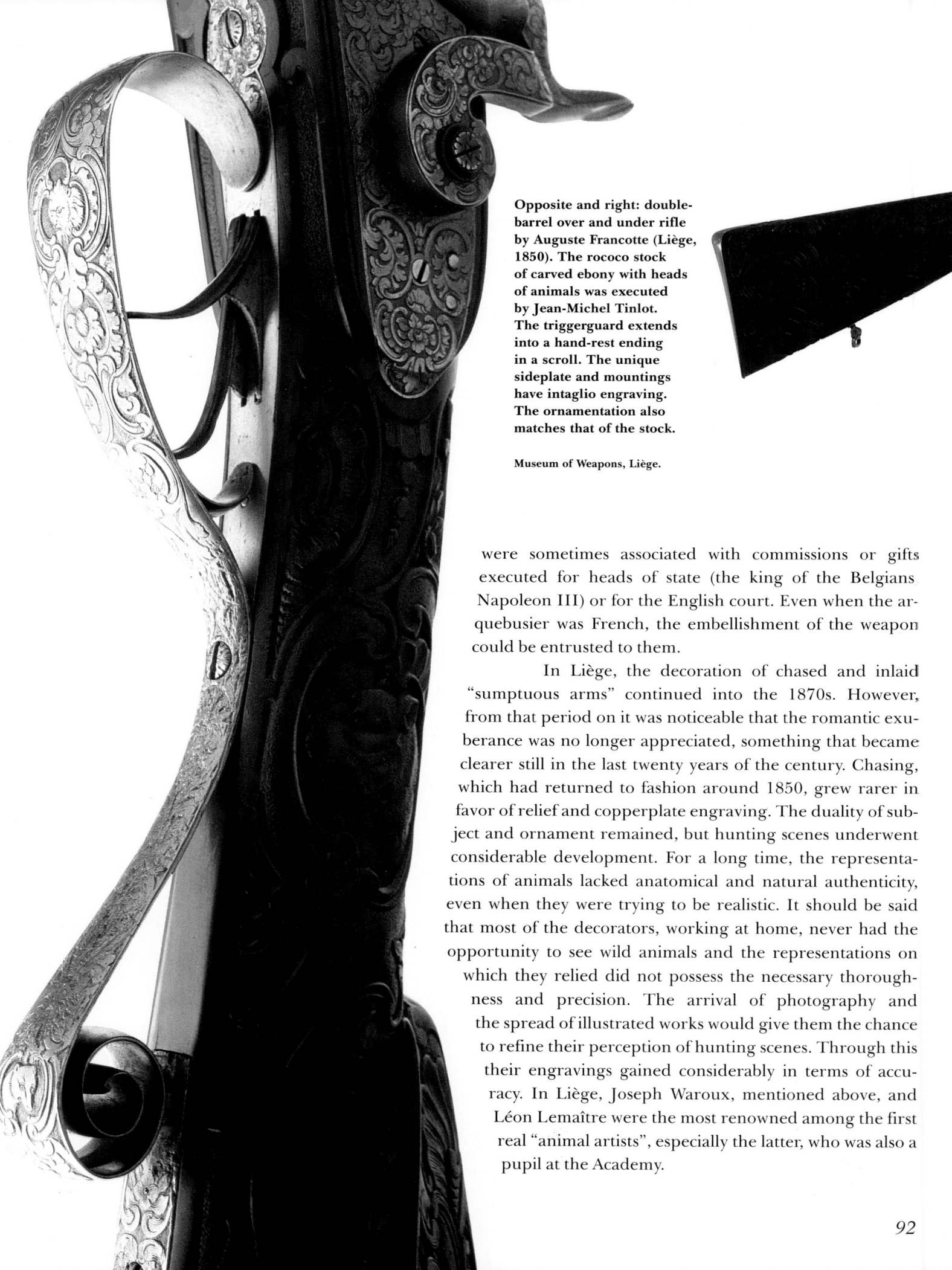

Opposite and right: double-barrel over and under rifle by Auguste Francotte (Liège, 1850). The rococo stock of carved ebony with heads of animals was executed by Jean-Michel Tinlot. The triggerguard extends into a hand-rest ending in a scroll. The unique sideplate and mountings have intaglio engraving. The ornamentation also matches that of the stock.

Museum of Weapons, Liège.

were sometimes associated with commissions or gifts executed for heads of state (the king of the Belgians, Napoleon III) or for the English court. Even when the arquebusier was French, the embellishment of the weapon could be entrusted to them.

In Liège, the decoration of chased and inlaid "sumptuous arms" continued into the 1870s. However, from that period on it was noticeable that the romantic exuberance was no longer appreciated, something that became clearer still in the last twenty years of the century. Chasing, which had returned to fashion around 1850, grew rarer in favor of relief and copperplate engraving. The duality of subject and ornament remained, but hunting scenes underwent considerable development. For a long time, the representations of animals lacked anatomical and natural authenticity, even when they were trying to be realistic. It should be said that most of the decorators, working at home, never had the opportunity to see wild animals and the representations on which they relied did not possess the necessary thoroughness and precision. The arrival of photography and the spread of illustrated works would give them the chance to refine their perception of hunting scenes. Through this their engravings gained considerably in terms of accuracy. In Liège, Joseph Waroux, mentioned above, and Léon Lemaître were the most renowned among the first real "animal artists", especially the latter, who was also a pupil at the Academy.

Opposite and above: double barrel Anson & Deeley system gun by Auguste Francotte (Liège, 1905). The hammers are internal. The recessed sideplates and the action have been finely engraved by Léon Lemaître (hunting scenes in the wild).

Museum of Weapons, Liège.

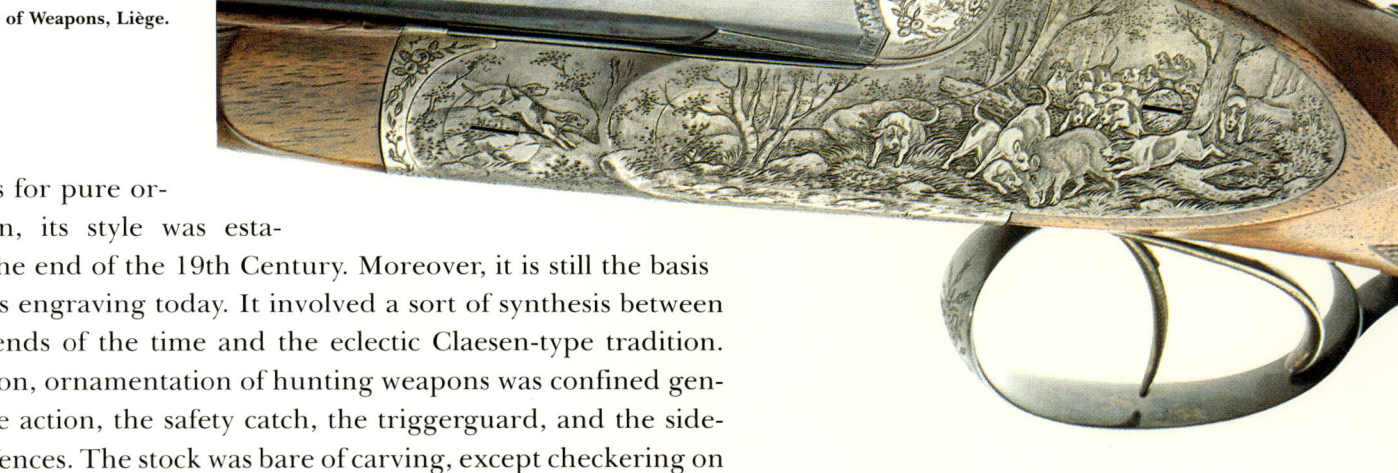

As for pure ornamentation, its style was established at the end of the 19th Century. Moreover, it is still the basis for weapons engraving today. It involved a sort of synthesis between the new trends of the time and the eclectic Claesen-type tradition. From then on, ornamentation of hunting weapons was confined generally to the action, the safety catch, the triggerguard, and the sideplates and fences. The stock was bare of carving, except checkering on the grip and light shaping behind the actions.

Vine and oak leaves, bindweed, as well as scrolls and chimeras remained in fashion, but it was the English engraving, with stylized lacey scrolls, which became increasingly widespread. The engravers from Liège combined this with their own elements: the Liénard scroll—a sort of Renaissance scroll sheathed in leaves—and in particular bouquets and ribbons. These ornaments, in Louis XVI style on a background of English engraving, were the specialty of the engraver Alphonse Delvenne, and his name remains associated with it.

93

Opposite and below: double-barrel 12-bore hammerless shotgun by Purdey & Sons, (1900). This gun was featured at the World Exposition of 1900 in Paris.

Museum of Weapons, Liège.

Great Britain

The British were the greatest innovators in hunting weapons in the 19th Century. The pragmatic character of this nation, which had often led it to favor the utilitarian and the functional, as well as a certain propensity to severity when it came to aesthetics, caused it to take very different routes in the luxury weapons field compared to those on the European continent. Thus, the British hunting weapon was characterized by its sobriety. With a few exceptions, the quest for maximum efficiency predominated. Here there were none of the ornamental extravagances generated in continental Europe by an unbridled romanticism. The distinctions awarded by the jury of the weaponry section at the World Exposition in Paris, in 1900, are revealing in this respect. Whereas the gold medal was given for a French weapon chased in the grand tradition of Napoleon III, contemporary English production had the last word in the grand prize: the Royal Hammerless Ejector Shotgun and the famous Paradox gun by Holland & Holland.

Since the first half of the Century, the embellishment of British guns had already been limited to large scrolls in copperplate or intaglio engraving (rarely chasing or gilding) applied to the lockplates. Subsequently, these motifs were engraved on the actions. The wooden areas were without flourishes, left clean, elegant, and with a simple checkering on the grip. Later on the scrolls became even more refined, ending up, around 1880, as minute scrolls evenly aligned, side by side, until they covered all the decorating surfaces. At the very start, this microscopic engraving or "lace", as it was known, had its detractors, because it was judged to be both fastidious and monotonous. But it became fully established and from the end of the century, "English

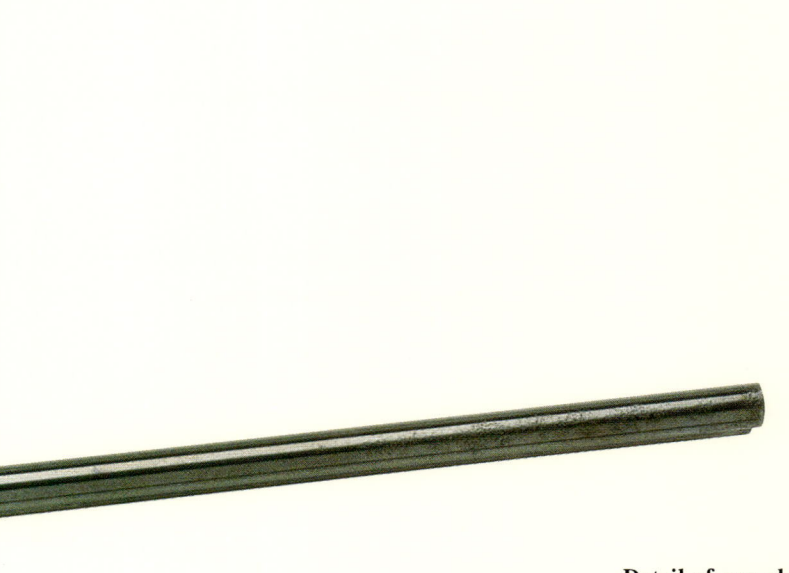

Detail of gun shown opposite: the lockplates and the ornaments in gray tempering are finely chased in Renaissance style: interwoven decorations of scrolls, mistletoe branches, chimeras, cupids and hunters.

engraving" became generally widespread and replaced other motifs or techniques, such as intaglio engraving and chasing in low relief, which were reserved henceforth for exceptional models.

This custom, insofar as it eventually influenced the weapons industry in the rest of Europe, resulted in the revival of more modest proportions in the fields of decoration and engraving, a trend from which Ferdinand Courally shirked in his *Treatise on hunting weapons and their shooting* (Paris, 1931): "It is not necessary for a rifle to be decorated, but the engraving does however have a use when its execution does not overburden the estimate of a sum which would be better spent if it was allocated to improving the quality of essential features." He estimated the sum spent on engraving to be between three and ten percent of the total price, a proportion which has changed since, as the cost of craftwork has increased considerably and the tendency to make luxury versions of certain products has continued to progress.

Also expressing the relative nature of ornamentation, David J. Baker wrote, in *The Royal Gunroom at Sandringham*, in connection with a .465 Express rifle of distinction, embellished with simple English bouquet engraving: "Without the slightest ostentation, of impeccably breeding but extremely powerful, this Purdey is the queen of the rifles at Sandringham. Despite its weight of 12 pounds, it is so well balanced that it appears light and only some external features betray the power of the cartridge for which is it chambered."

American Winchester rifle, Model 1866. The action is in bronze, decorated with engraved scrolls, and bears the name of the owner.

Museum of Hunting and Natural History, Paris.

The United States of America

Even though it cannot be said that the United States was among the "greats" of weapons ornamentation in the 19th Century, a place should nevertheless be reserved for America because of the particular decorative style which originated there. Firearms have played a very important role in the history of this country. Dependant on immigration to enrich and diversify their human resources, Americans were for a long time reliant on gunmakers coming from abroad. Inventors of mass production, they manufactured large quantities of weapons that were strictly utilitarian and whose intended use was not necessarily the shooting of game, even where civilian weapons were concerned. The only known embellishments before the middle of the 19th Century were scrolls in German or English style, applied in or out of the factory on certain pistols and shoulder weapons.

However, around 1850 the need arose to make luxury versions of certain mass-produced weapons to sell to more demanding individuals or for presentation to important figures in the country or abroad. It was the German immigrants arriving around this time who created, from various elements, a true school of American engraving to respond to this demand. Louis D. Nimschke (1832-1904) worked mostly in New York, where he practiced a style of engraving characterized by wide, shadowed scroll, executed in shallow-cut style, on matte or hatched backgrounds, sometimes accompanied by animal heads or typically American hunting and riding scenes. Another influential

Details of the rifle shown left. The engraving depicts a chamois hunt and a stag, surrounded by flowering and leafy scrolls, and a gun dog at the heel of the buttplate. The butt contains the cleaning equipment in a compartment with a removable lid.

engraver of German origin, Gustave Young, established himself in Hartford and then in Springfield. He worked especially for Colt (pistols), but also for other manufacturers. He, and his sons Oscar and Eugène after him, created scrolls using intaglio engraving and gold inlay. Finally, the brothers Conrad F. (1844-1925) and John Ulrich (1850-1924), established in Hartford and New Haven, were the start of a true dynasty of engravers of whom the last was to die in 1949. Working for Winchester, they practiced the usual neo-Renaissance scrolls but resolved the problem created by the wide decorating surfaces on repeating weapons by dividing them into compartments through the juxtaposition of medallions that were shallow-cut or sometimes in copperplate-engraving.

At the end of the century, there was evidence of a growing craze for black bronzed backgrounds in intaglio engraving or embellished with subjects inlaid in gold. In the same way, in the top-of-the range models, carving on the stocks enjoyed a certain popularity. In some cases, the grip and the handguard were decorated quite heavily with geometric motifs and interlacing.

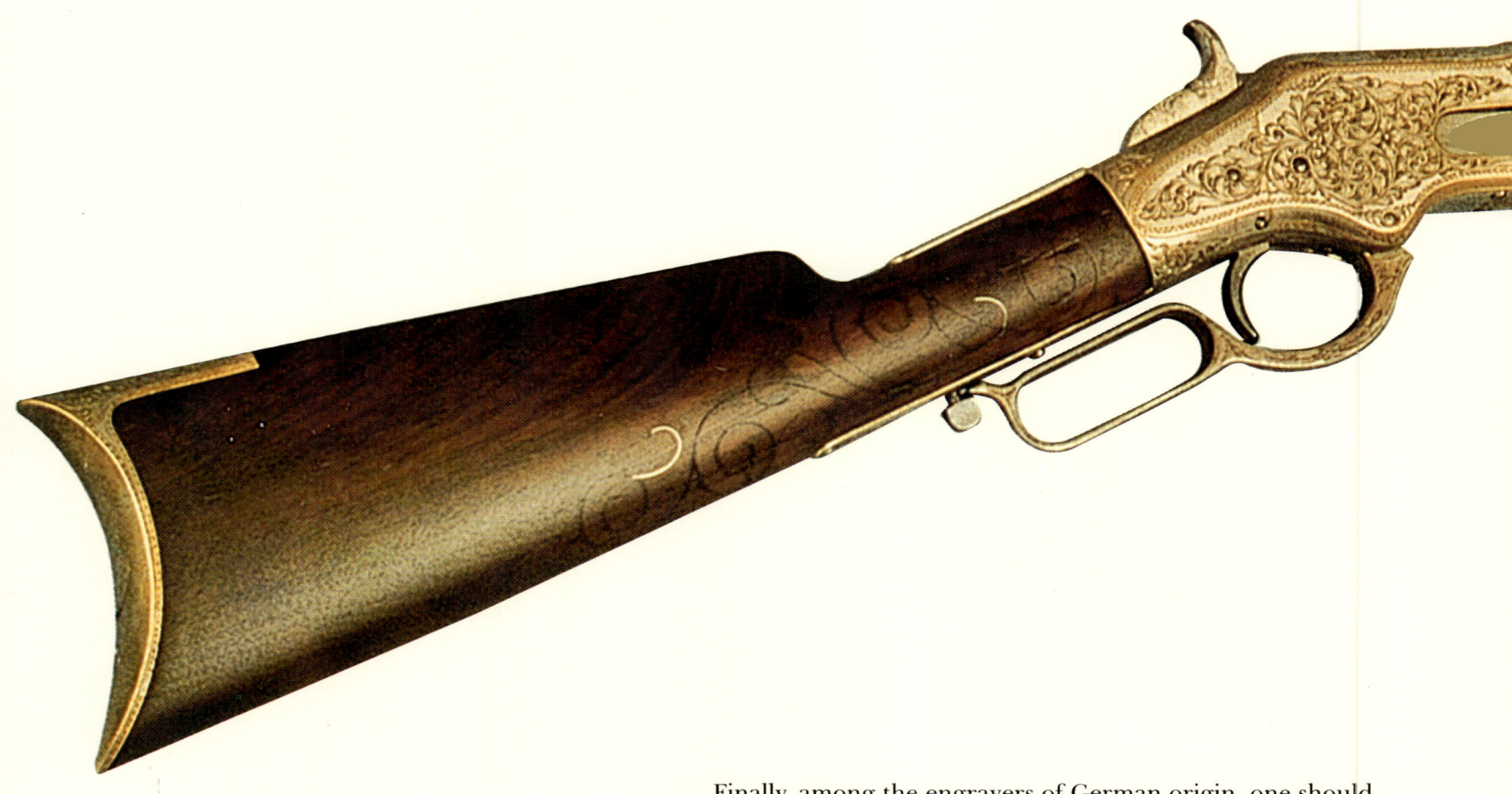

Above and right: Winchester 1866 carbine, caliber .44 RF (rimfire). Exquisite breech in silver, decorated with shadowed scrolls, typical of the work of the famous engraver Louis D. Nimschke. The weapon was made in 1872. On the left side can be seen the ring which allows the carbine to be hooked onto a saddle.

Finally, among the engravers of German origin, one should also mention Cuno A. Helfricht, who, having served is apprenticeship in Berlin, worked exclusively for Colt from 1871 until his retirement in 1921.

None of these New World engravers, however, had broken off communications with Europe, whether they were newly arrived immigrants or long established across the Atlantic. Their sources of inspiration remained linked to the Old Continent. The ornaments that they used and adapted, and the mythological personifications of which their public remained fond, were derived from ancient archetypes. The books of designs had also remained in current use among them. Whereas the documentary sources and the conceptual references remained European, the theme set moved away from the old masters. The engraved subjects proved to be well and truly American—the game, the hunting scenes and the characters depicted testified to a way of life and to new horizons that were giving pride of place to a sort of cult of the life in open air, the *outdoor life*.

If we have ended with the specific ornamentation of American weapons, it is less by reason of its intrinsic value than by its subsequent influence on weapons decoration in the world. In fact, its stereotypical motifs in the form of wide scrolls, its representations of game, the use of gold inlay and its somewhat ostentatious character are just the elements which in turn were to influence the European weapons industry in the mid-20th Century.

Other Countries

Other countries had, of course, continued to engrave and embellish hunting weapons during the 19th Century. The styles in fashion in France, Belgium and England predominated there, with local characteristics accentuated to a greater or lesser extent. The neo-styles were also practiced, but with a few exceptions they did not arouse the same passion.

The German region remained faithful to its taste for weighty decoration. A nostalgia for the "horror of emptiness" of earlier times revealed a great mastery of form and matter, even if the decoration was not in the most delicate of taste.

Greatly influenced by this eclecticism of styles, Anton Vinzent Lebeda, from Prague, and his sons Anton and Ferdinand, both also engravers, who took over the firm on the death of their father (1857), had a particularly outstanding body of work that, in terms of decoration, could rival that of the great artists of Europe. They excelled in intaglio engraving and damascene work, as well as the carving of stocks. In addition to the

100

Detail of the weapon shown below. It was presented to a German general by a corps of Austrian officers. On the damascus barrels, executed by Jérôme Flachat, from Saint-Etienne, can be seen all their names.

Museum of Weapons, Liège.

"gothic" pistol, as well as the designs exploiting the theme of the hunter eaten by hares (that were reproduced in the collection of Claesen), we are indebted to them for several top-of-the-range guns still preserved today. At the chateau of Fuschl, near Salzburg, there is a beautiful percussion weapon with over and under barrels that has finely engraved plates and a stock entirely carved with Louis XIV scrolls on a checkered background (c. 1860). The museum of Weapons in Liège also has a gun with rich engraving and damascene work that was presented to a general from Baden in 1857 to mark the jubilee of his military career.

Farther east, the work of a Polish engraver established in Warsaw between 1861 and 1880, Jan Jachimek, is worthy of attention. In particular we are indebted to him for the decoration of two very finely worked guns from the early 1860s. One, kept at the Hermitage Museum in St.Petersburg, has over and under barrels. The sideplates, in blued steel, are decorated with chased hunting scenes surrounded by damascene work. The hammers, in a style showing hints of gothic, are also damascened as are the barrels and the chased cartridge box in the butt. The latter is carved and inlaid with copper scrolls. The second weapon belongs to the museum of Weapons in Liege.

Above and left: double-barrel shotgun by Anton and Ferdinand Lebeda (Prague, 1857), 12 bore. The stock is carved and studded with silver. The chasing and the damascene work, great specialties of the Lebeda brothers, are magnificent. Detail on the plate shows trophies and a bivouac, as well as an allegorical figure on the hammer. The chasing on the triggerguard depicts two servicemen.

Museum of Weapons, Liège.

Percussion hunting weapon made by Jachimek and Sosnowski, of Warsaw (c. 1860). The chased medallion depicts Casimir Pulaski, the hero of Polish and American independence in the 18th Century.

Museum of Weapons, Liège.

102

Detail of the weapon shown left. The stock is inlaid with Polish characters in traditional costume. On the left, Stephan Czarniecki, conqueror of the Muscovite army in 1660; on the right, Tadeusz Kosciuszko, hero of Polish and American independence in the 18th Century. Below: detail of the hammer.

Finally, in Russia, the production of hunting weapons continued among some gunmakers and at the factory at Toula. The characteristics conformed to the Western models that they also imported in large quantities for a well-off clientele. Some weapons were decorated with a certain heaviness in the traditional taste: carved stocks, engraving, inlay using various metals, sometimes chasing.

On the whole, the closing 19th Century ended with an international style of arms-making, with models that were more or less standardized and spread worldwide, and decorative choices in which the regional characteristics tended to become blurred but did not really disappear.

Around 1900, the hunting gun and even the rifle were adorned with an ornamentation that was usually limited to engraving the sideplates or the action and the trigger guard. The motifs were generally Renaissance scrolls, garlands and ribbons, leaves or English style "tapestry" scrolls, and sometimes chimeras. The stock work, in walnut, was limited to checkering, sometimes with moldings around the action; this rarely bore true sculptures, except in the countries of central and eastern Europe or perhaps the United States. Presentation weapons also had a tendency to fall into line with these criteria. In all cases they avoided the extravagances of former times. Optimal functionality, purification of tastes and standardization of manufacture resulted in a fineness and a kind of aesthetic modesty which left the engravers with an increasingly narrow and difficult field in which to exercise their talents.

THE 20TH CENTURY

Grand classic from the house of Purdey in the 1890s, with bar-action locks. The purity of the lines of the hammers and the delicate engraving illustrate the epitome of British hammerguns at the dawn of the 20th Century.

This gun from the house of Purdey dates from the 1870s. The delicate tapestry engraving, based on stylized scrolls, becomes the characteristic of English weapons decoration in this period.

Until the end of the 19th Century, the arms industry was composed of two major sectors: the craft workshops, which produced weapons for hunting, self-defense and sport shooting, and the manufacturers that produced weapons of war. The engraving workshops were also extremely versatile. Craftsmen created and executed engravings, chasing and inlay on weapons and also on jewelry and sometimes on plates, of copper and steel, for publication or as the original drawings of etchings… However, the arrival of industrialization enabled the military sector to reduce the manufacturing time of weapons while still maintaining a certain standard of quality. Mechanical investment was barely affordable by the majority of craftsmen who had to work within these new structures of production, while those few who possessed the means built modern weapons factories. At the start of the 20th Century, these economic changes caused the near disappearance of many artistic professions and of workshops that dated from the Renaissance. The engravers had to adapt themselves to the demands of production. They specialized, one in jewelry, another in weapons, another in printing…

The English reference

In England, towards the end of the 19th Century, massive industrialization surpassed other countries. The introduction of the machine tool was of paramount importance, especially in the field of precision manufacturing. Furthermore, English gunmakers had

Double-barrel Dickson gun, Anson system. The exquisite English bouquet decoration dates from 1910-1920.

invented new hunting weapons that were much better suited to "pre-mechanization", such as the "hammerless" (internal-hammer) sidelock gun and the Anson & Deeley boxlock gun, which concentrated the mechanical action near the balance point.

The most important innovations in the sporting arms were henceforth to come from England.

At the beginning of the 20th Century, prestigious firms such as Holland & Holland, Purdey, Boss, Westley Richards, Woodward, Churchill, Dickson, Lancaster, Grant and others produced the most beautiful and the most reliable shotguns and rifles in the world. The demand for these prestige weapons came above all from a limited circle of connoisseurs, British subjects for the most part, who had made their fortunes from the exploitation of vast areas in the colonies.

Side-by-side double gun by J. Woodward & Sons. The stained-glass-style chiselwork on the fences (behind the barrels) is outstanding.

The great English gunmakers, however, had to resolve a number of problems, in particular in relation to the choice of materials and ammunition, because the majority of rifles ordered were intended for hunting larger animals than those found in Europe. Whereas mass production from then on was rational and utilized precision machine tools (involving the redesign of the external archi-

Purdey gun from the beginning of the 20th Century, decorated with English engraving.

tecture of the weapon), these classical gunmakers continued to call on different specialists, in particular for the balance and line of the weapon, the finishing and the stockwork. They selected the best pieces of French walnut from the Périgord region and cut them to preserve the beautiful grain. The wood had to be as dense as possible in the butt section, for strength, and the grain had to run parallel through the smooth line of the grip. In general, fine walnut could only be used after a period of some seven years, the average length of time needed for natural drying. Into these precious pieces of wood were fitted the mechanical elements of the gun (perfectly made and polished to a mirror-finish) and the buttstock and forend themselves were precisely shaped to the dimensions of the owner and for his or her style of shooting.

The stock, carefully smoothed with sandpaper and then hand-rubbed with an oil sealer and finish, took on the characteristic warm honey glow of a fine English gun. The grip and forend were delicately and conservatively decorated with checkering, a pattern of intersecting lines cut into the wood that provided a secure grip. English gunmakers had long before ceased to embellish their stocks with carving; they preferred to let the material and the fine lines of the work express their natural beauty.

Side-by-side Boss gun with English bouquet engraving, a popular standard between 1915-1925.

They tempered the mechanical parts in places subject to the most friction and breakage. Finally, they case-hardened the surfaces of the action and the sideplates as well as the furnishings. Then the final fitting and finishing was carried out, essential after the heat and chemical treatments. The result of all this was an extraordinary harmony of lines and colors.

In addition, English gunmakers showed their genius for harmonizing technology with beauty and creativity. Faced with unusual decorating surfaces, they had to innovate in the field of engraving. It should not be forgotten that English engraving, after the second half of the 19th Century, always referred back to French pre-romantic engraving. Nevertheless, one could already detect in it the first signs of its originality. The English engravers also drew their inspiration from certain French and English manuscripts such as the *Roman de la Rose*, by Guillaume de Lorris and Jean de Meung (13thC), or the *Canterbury Tales* by Chaucer (15thC). On the borders that frame the frontispieces of these books there can be seen geometric designs and elegant bouquets of flowers and leaves around which unfold delicate and ethereal scrolls.

This type of decoration would go on to be found on numerous English weapons at the end of the 19th Century and the beginning of the 20th Century, a period when the engravers began once again to really get a taste for decorating beautiful hunting weapons.

They adapted the pre-romantic style of French engraving to their taste by reducing and further refining the scrolls of foliage inter-

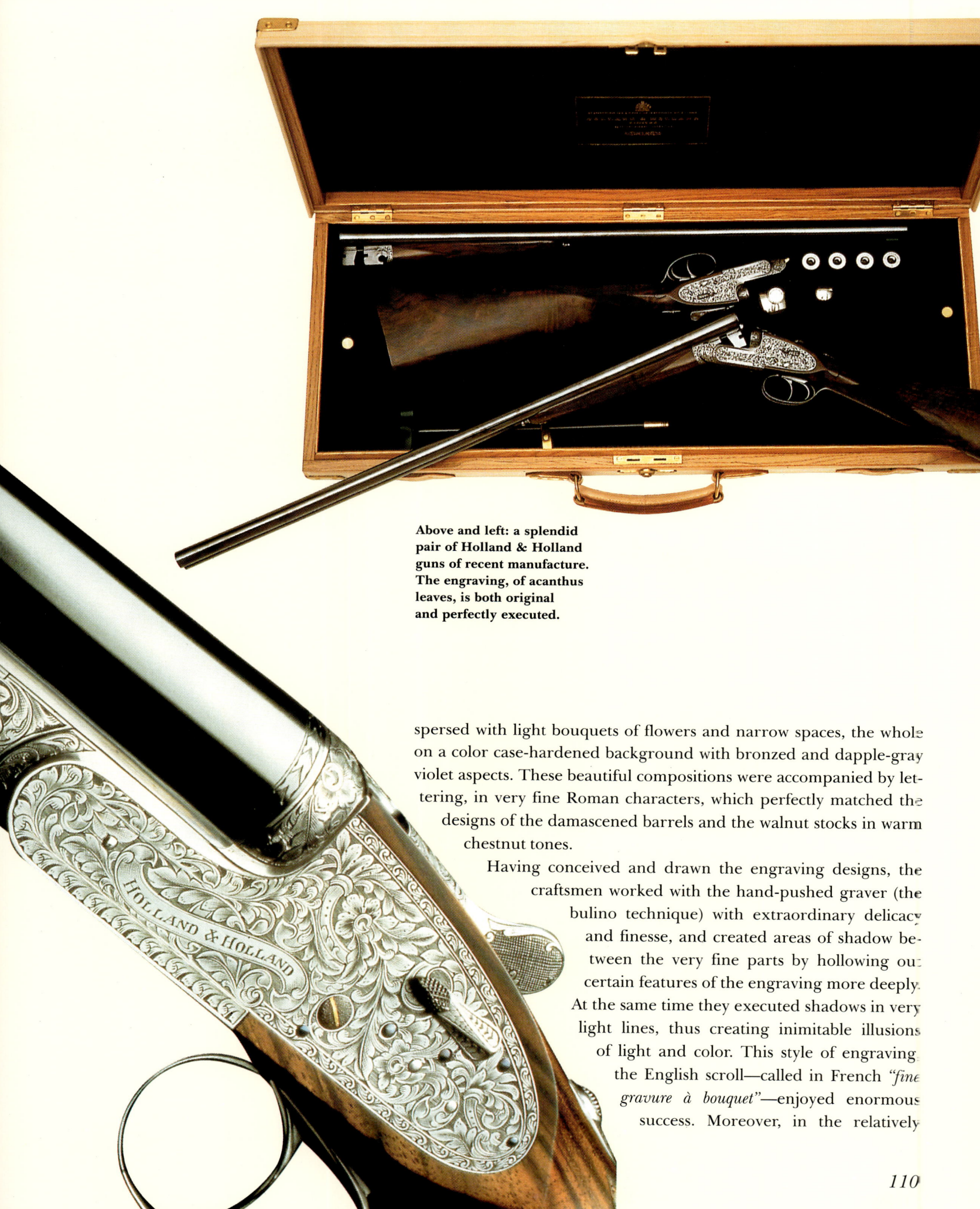

Above and left: a splendid pair of Holland & Holland guns of recent manufacture. The engraving, of acanthus leaves, is both original and perfectly executed.

spersed with light bouquets of flowers and narrow spaces, the whole on a color case-hardened background with bronzed and dapple-gray violet aspects. These beautiful compositions were accompanied by lettering, in very fine Roman characters, which perfectly matched the designs of the damascened barrels and the walnut stocks in warm chestnut tones.

Having conceived and drawn the engraving designs, the craftsmen worked with the hand-pushed graver (the bulino technique) with extraordinary delicacy and finesse, and created areas of shadow between the very fine parts by hollowing out certain features of the engraving more deeply. At the same time they executed shadows in very light lines, thus creating inimitable illusions of light and color. This style of engraving, the English scroll—called in French *"fine gravure à bouquet"*—enjoyed enormous success. Moreover, in the relatively

standardized middle-grade weapons the style of engraving remained of French or English inspiration throughout Europe, with the exception of the Germanic countries and Spain, which retained their respective traditions.

Unfortunately the names of the artists who executed these engravings remain largely unknown. At that time the name of the maker was of prime importance. For each company and for each model of weapon produced, a specific engraving was conceived. The model then became a standard that illustrated the sales catalogs of each firm.

It should not be forgotten that the best English firms created, and still create, apart from these fabulous standard models, custom-made hunting weapons as well. They are generally presented to leading world figures or sold to the most demanding clients.

From top to bottom: Mythological hunting scene engraved on a recent Holland & Holland shotgun.

Plate engraved by Philippe Grifnée, on a Holland & Holland gun, depicting an episode in the American Civil War.

Hunting scene in English style, inlaid in different shades of gold and shaded using the bulino technique, on a Holland & Holland gun.

The floral engraving on this sidelock gun is the work of Hippolite Corombelle (1871-1943), one of the forerunners of present-day Belgian engraving.

Museum of Weapons, Liège.

Beretta shotgun from the 1950s engraved by Lyson Corombelle (1894-1971), son of Hippolite. This scene is representative of the style of these great engravers.

Beretta archives.

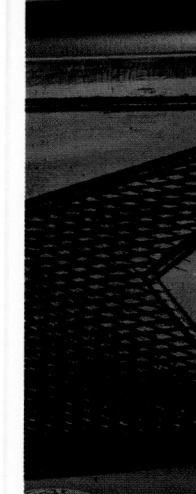

The evolution of engraving in the 20th Century

With the scroll of the English engravers gaining widespread acceptance, Art Nouveau had little influence on weapons engraving, although this was not the case among the Belgian engravers (Delvenne first, then Corombelle and his son Lyson), who were very sensitive to this decorative art. They created the most beautiful engravings in the form of intertwined garlands and winding ribbons on a tapestry background of very delicate scrolls. This also became a very famous style. However, the weapons makers of Liège, those who were manufacturing high-quality hunting weapons, had prejudices which they could not overcome. Having forgotten the example of the arquebusiers of the past, they established a norm according to which the price of the engraving would not exceed one quarter of the value of a weapon. Furthermore, to justify their calculations, they claimed that too much engraving only served to hide the faults in items badly produced by less than scrupulous gunmakers.

As this bizarre mode of reasoning was widely held in the world of weaponry, it contributed significantly to bringing about the decline of the engraving profession (to a certain extent) everywhere in Europe. Corombelle, to name but one, was forced to go into "exile" in Italy for a time, to Beretta. This sad situation lasted until well after the Second World War, and the trend accelerated in the 1960s with the proliferating use of machine tools for manufacturing everything and anything.

And so, for the engravers, this was another of their darkest periods. They were reduced to doing inexpensive work, executing engravings using the repetitive stamping technique and touching up certain features made by machine. Many were forced to abandon their profession to work on the production line in the factories. Only some engravers and some master gunsmakers found a way to resist and to keep alive the taste for the artistic hunting weapon.

At the end of the '60s, one of them, the Italian Mario Abbiatico, felt that the time was ripe to relaunch fine hunting weapons. So he founded his own business with Salvinelli, a gunmaker of quality who was a very good designer. Unfortunately, by then it had become very

Browning A5 shotgun engraved by Félix Funken in 1936. The style is clearly influenced by the Art deco movement of the period between the wars.

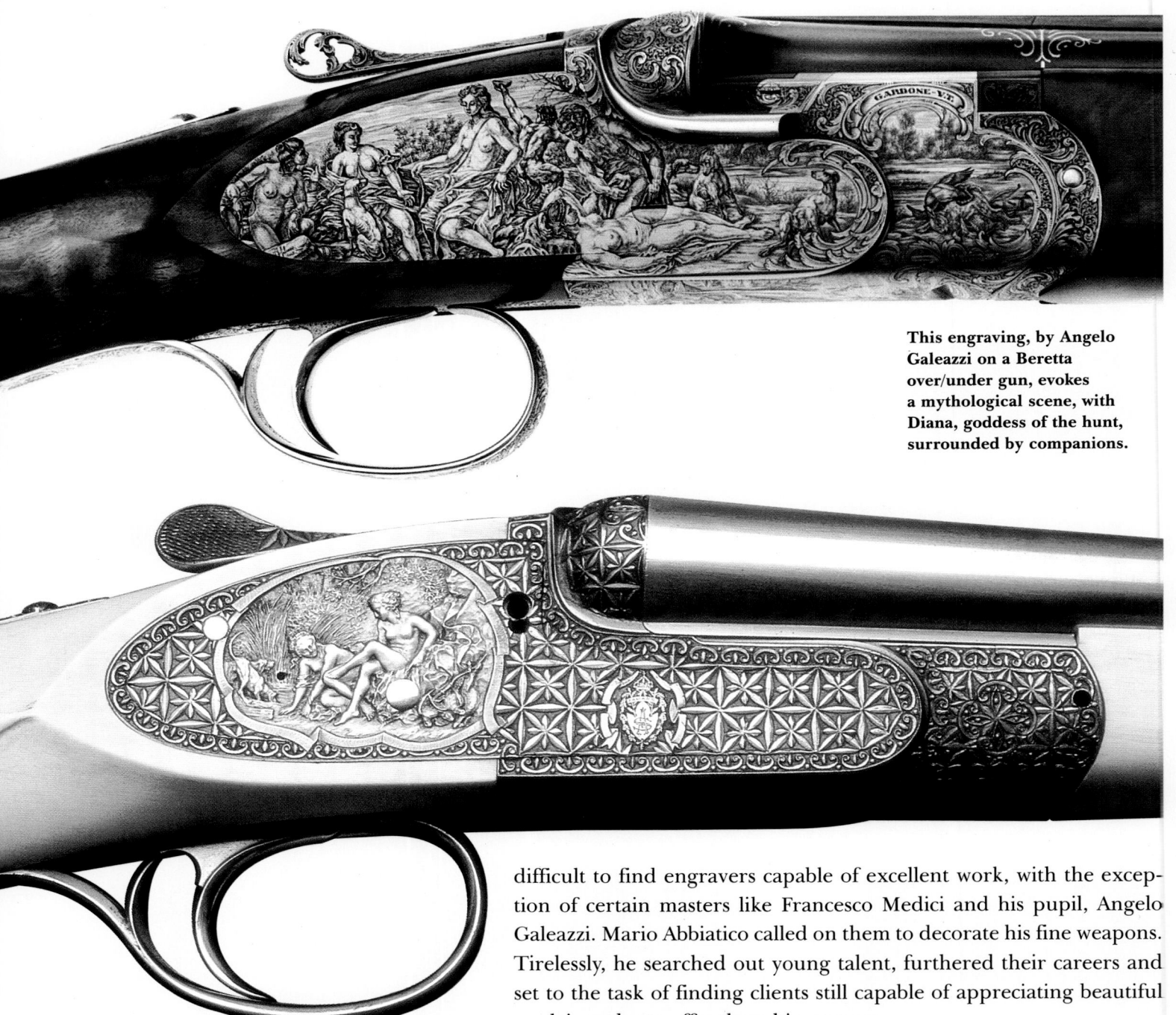

This engraving, by Angelo Galeazzi on a Beretta over/under gun, evokes a mythological scene, with Diana, goddess of the hunt, surrounded by companions.

On this Abbiatico & Salvinelli double gun, the chasing is the work of Francesco Medici. It is an outstanding example of the work of this artist, who was the forerunner of present-day engraving on hunting weapons in Italy. The stock and forend are ivory.

difficult to find engravers capable of excellent work, with the exception of certain masters like Francesco Medici and his pupil, Angelo Galeazzi. Mario Abbiatico called on them to decorate his fine weapons. Tirelessly, he searched out young talent, furthered their careers and set to the task of finding clients still capable of appreciating beautiful work in order to offer them his weapons.

For his own part, Galeazzi, in executing magnificent engravings inspired by the creative example of the Renaissance, gradually developed his own style. He became the trend-setter followed by young engravers.

In the '70s, one of them, Firmo Fracassi, who had a highly individual style and a fantastic creative ability, caused a real revolution in the art of engraving by inventing a completely new manner of expression. This artist also acquired many emulators in Italy and internationally.

This sudden revival in quality engraving gave Mario Abbiatico the idea to create and publish a book, *Grandi Incisioni su armi*

**From left to right:
Mario Abbiatico, founder
of the house of Salvinelli.**

**The engraver Angelo Galeazzi
in his workshop.**

**The master Giulio Timpini
flanked by two pupils at
the Beretta school of engraving.**

d'oggi ("Great engraving on Today's Weapons"), a reference work which has been reprinted many times.

In Italy, during the last twenty years, numerous talents have been discovered. Gianfranco Pedersoli executes ornamental engravings of his own design that have an ideal balance between flora and fauna. Giancarlo Pedretti and his son Stefano are specialists in portraits of gun dogs and people, and even historical monuments that certain clients wish to immortalize on their weapons. These two engravers decorate the weapons of some of the English firms such as Purdey. The engraver Terzi expresses himself by using fantastic and futuristic characters that combine feminine bodies with animals and grotesque masks—a highly evocative and provocative mix. As for Manrico Torcoli, his imagination and creativity combined with an impressive skill make him a real phenomenon.

The "Bottega Incisione" of Cesare Giovanelli, which was founded around ten years ago, offers the most advanced technical experience in the field of engraving instruction, in particular on

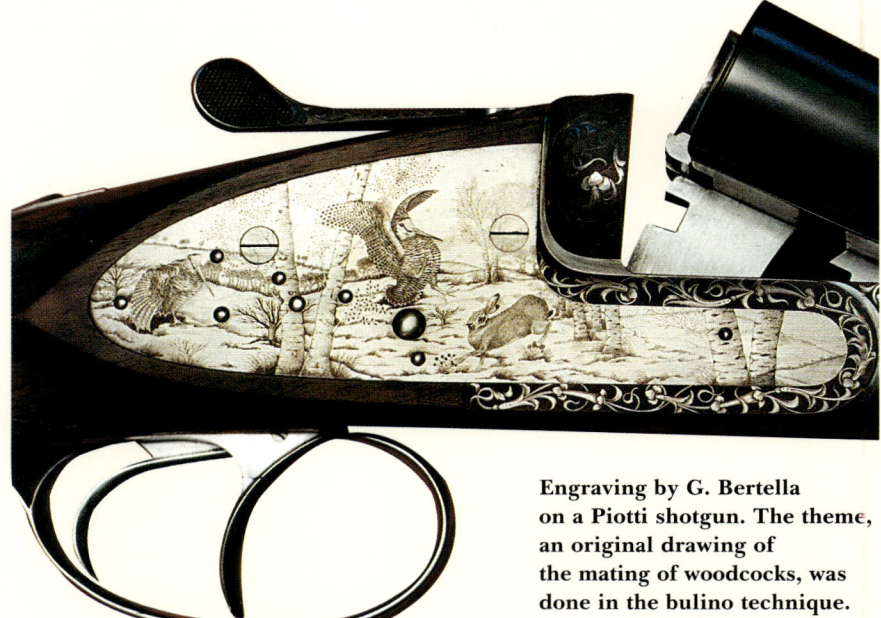

Engraving by G. Bertella on a Piotti shotgun. The theme, an original drawing of the mating of woodcocks, was done in the bulino technique.

Impressive animal scenes engraved by Angelo Galeazzi. The animals and vegetation are inlaid in fine gold on a double-barrel Express rifle.

weapons. Its doctrine is based on three fundamental elements: the teaching of drawing, manual training in the various engraving techniques, and the stimulation of the individual creativity of each pupil. This international school is free and open to all, but the number of pupils is limited. Cesare Giovanelli also has shops that offer mechanical engraving and another shop for manual engraving, which has about fifteen employees. The best pupils in his school may, if they wish, become employees of this business at the end of their course.

The Beretta firm has maintained at the heart of its operation an important manual engraving shop for professionals and has recently opened a teaching workshop to train young artisans. These operations are run by Giulio Timpini, an engraver of vast experience who is also a teacher.

In Belgium, the FN (Fabrique Nationale) engraving shop, created in 1926 (and which has had as many as 180 engravers), as well as the school of weapons, in Liège, has helped continue a profession that, without them would have perished. It is as a result of this that Louis Vrancken left behind original engravings in a very personal style. Familiar with the whole range of engraving techniques, Vrancken knew how to combine creativity with faultless execution. He was the most important en-

Express rifle by Ludwig Borovnik engraved by Hans Oblitschnig. This is a superb example of the Austrian style of chasing.

Detail of a Browning shotgun engraved by Louis Vrancken. The scene and the fine surround are inlaid in gold. The birds in intaglio engraving are typical of the Belgian school of engraving.

graver in Belgium in the 1960s and '70s, as had previously been Félix Funken (founder of the FN engraving shop), André Watrin, his successor, and Lyson Corombelle, son of Hippolite. Currently, Lovenberg, Grifnée and Baerten figure among the best Belgian engravers.

In France, tribute should be paid to the engraver Christian Freycon for his creative talent, his style and his capacity to employ the whole range of engraving techniques in executing work of the highest standard. No longer living, he created engravings particularly for the Granger firm, which remains the best French maker of artistic weapons. His pieces figure among the most beautiful in the world.

In England, the engraver Kenneth Hunt still maintains, with his son and daughter, an outstanding level of engraving work. As do the Brown brothers and Philip Coggan.

In Austria, there are also excellent engravers such as Johann Singer and Hans Obiltschnig. At Ferlach, there is an engraving school in which the best artisans work in a somewhat traditional style, characterized by ornamentation based on oak leaves, edelweiss and wild thistles and by scenes depicting the alpine animals hunted in Austria. They also produce scenes of large African game on weapons intended for this type of hunting. The execution of their engraving is relatively deep, forming low reliefs that are neo-gothic in character.

Top-of-the-line Beretta shotgun, decorated with extremely meticulous engraving.

The house of Piotti. Stockmaker at his bench.

The fine-gun business today

The influence of English gunmakers was a determining factor in the course of the 20th Century, and the English companies still impose their style. The most important gunmakers in the world continue to take their inspiration from these great standards. At stake, is the goal of creating the most perfect gun—finding more effective mechanical solutions and better ballistic performance while still contributing individual solutions in terms of aesthetics.

Today, the production centers of fine weapons in Europe have undergone some changes. Since the 1930s, even the best English firms, faced with the shortage of specialized labor, have not been spared, and many have been forced to merge with large firms. Through such consolidations the quality of the classic British game gun has been maintained.

The fine-gun businesses of Liège have experienced difficulties in the course of the last thirty years also. Prestigious firms have disappeared after failing to understand the importance of investing in new, and now indispensable, technology. Only firms such as Lebeau-Courally, Francotte and Dumoulin have been able to survive, alongside Browning, a subsidiary of the Herstal S.A. group. In contrast, a new company to build fine hunting weapons has been created by Marcel Thys, a former teacher at the school of weapons in Liège.

Several examples of current production at Abbiatico & Salvinelli.

Belgian "Nemrod" double-barrel gun manufactured in Liège by Lebeau-Courally.

In France, the situation has also deteriorated, with the disappearance of Manufrance and the collapse of many highly skilled artisan gunmaking companies. Today, alongside weapons industries such as Verney-Carron and middle-sized businesses like Chapuis Armes, craftsmen such as Granger, Savin, Redon, Ripamonti, Geffrois, Périn or Paul Chapuis are surviving and again producing weapons of high quality.

In Germany, with its large weapons industry, one can still find a high quality small marker of fine hunting weapons, Hartmann & Weis.

In Austria, the artisan gunmakers have sensibly founded a cooperative of precision tools at Ferlach, which provides each of them the mechanization necessary to achieve a high technological standard in order to producing beautiful hunting weapons, especially rifles. Among the best-known are Borovnik, Chiring and Pramesberger.

Finally, in Italy, alongside Beretta, the largest industrial manufacturer of top-of-the-range hunting arms, can be found workshops which produce fine hunting and artistic guns of incomparable quality—names such as Fabbri, Rizzini, Piotti, Desenzani, Abbiatico & Salvinelli, Bertuzzi, Bosis, Zanotti, Toschi and Cortisi.

The most recent phenomenon is the growing number of American engravers, some of a very high standard, who exercise their profession in the United States, where the demand for sporting weapons remains very high.

PORTRAITS OF ENGRAVERS

Engraver's workbench in the Piotti workshops.

Philip Coggan

England, *20th Century*

Born in 1948 in Wales, Philip Coggan, a professional decorator and painter and also a lover and collector of artistic weaponry, has a particular enthusiasm for their decoration. For about a decade, Coggan made copies of braces of early flintlock dueling pistols.

It was through his visits to gunmakers, arms collectors and English and Italian engravers that he was eventually able to devote himself professionally to this mode of artistic expression.

Completely self-taught, he succeeded in penetrating and mastering the secrets of engraving. Today, he has become one of the most outstanding figures of English engraving.

He is also recognized worldwide, and his work is commissioned by the most famous firms, such as Holland & Holland, and by a demanding private clientele. Coggan is best known for his animal scenes and his portraits of people.

Coggan is renowned for his engravings of people. These, executed on a Holland & Holland shotgun, represent the English royal family. The detail below shows the figure of Lord Mountbatten.

Creative Art

Italy, 20th Century

Mythological scene of Diana, the goddess of the hunt, finely engraved and framed by romantic ornamentation. This work was executed on a L.Bosis gun and was inspired by a Watteau painting.

The Creative Art workshop is made up of five engravers: Valerio Peli, Giacomo Fausti, Armando Piardi, Giovanni Steduto and Ugo Talenti. They all attended the Cesare Giovanelli school of engraving, where they benefited from the teaching of Campanelli, a highly talented artist and painter. They also learned to use the different techniques for engraving on weapons and on precious metals, to master the burin, the hammer and bulino engraving in order to execute line-engraving, recessed backgrounds, chasing, decorations with and on precious metals as well as techniques for creating printing plates. They then practiced their profession individually for several years and gained considerable experience.
One day they decided to start afresh, and Creative Art was born.
On entering this workshop, it is surprising to find the sort of atmosphere that prevailed in the humanist workshops of the Renaissance. The flow and organization of work is managed in an egalitarian and democratic fashion. The engravers work on projects and decide prices together. Sometimes, for important orders for themed engraving such as, for example, a series dedicated to the work of Michelangelo, they will carry out the work jointly.
In the space of six years, Creative Art has succeeding in winning the appreciation of a clientele of connoisseurs throughout the world.

The dramatic effect of this scene engraved on a Piotti shotgun is striking. The frame of delicate English-style work surrounds the exquisite embellishments and the eagle's head.

Hunting scene magnificently executed using the bulino technique. Here, reality gives way to make-believe.

Partial view of the Creative Art workshop: benches with equipment and revolving vises used for engraving while standing, a classic technique in Italy, especially for the engraving of firearms.

Ornamental engraving in classic Renaissance style, executed on a recessed background and with shadowing using the bulino technique; on a Piotti double shotgun.

Firmo Fracassi

Italy, 20th Century

Born in 1939 in a little village in the province of Brescia, in the north of Italy, Firmo Fracassi has been an enthusiast of artistic design since his adolescence. Self-taught, he studied history of art and took an interest in the study of anatomy, perspective and the effects of light and shadow. His aim was to embrace the knowledge of the grand masters of the Renaissance in order to create his own style.
His meeting with Mario Abbiatico enabled engraving to reach heights unthinkable before the mid-1960s. Fracassi is astounding in all fields of engraving: chasing on firearms, jewelry, knives ... Always striving for technical perfection, Fracassi sharpens his burins in a highly tapered V-shape, at an angle of 60 to 70 degrees (the norm being 40 to 45 degrees), in order to engrave lines

Engraved lockplate on the theme of Bonaparte's Egyptian campaign, on an Abbiatico & Salvinelli shotgun. The execution is exceptional because the interplay of shadows brings out perfectly the dramatic effect of the battle.

An episode in Bonaparte's Italian campaign engraved on a lockplate. The tonalities of shadow are outstanding.

Engraving of a hunting scene on a Beretta over/under gun executed using the bulino technique: pointers and a duck.

of decreasing length that finally became a dot. This technique enables him to chisel the material deeply while keeping the line very narrow and, depending on the distances, to create a spectrum of shadows ranging from deepest black through various shades of gray to white. As the light absorbed this way cannot be reflected in this type of line, the artist is able to vary the effects of light and shadow to an extreme degree, creating the impression of three-dimensional volume. The creative work of Fracassi can appear very classical at first sight. However, closer examination reveals a distinct humanist sensitivity, composed of questions about the meaning of life. In observing the structure of landscapes, vegetation and in particular trees, it is impossible not to be entranced. In the animal scenes, Fracassi knows exactly how to freeze movement to compose a picture. His grotesque characters are of the sort that have reflected the particular taste of Brescian engraving since classical times. The masks executed by Firmo Fracassi, usually on a background of ornamentation reminiscent of Art nouveau style, are full of distant memories of tales and myths.

For many years, Fracassi has worked directly with private clients. After discussing with them the general idea for the engraving, he reflects for about three months and prepares a project plan which he submits to each client. Thus, each time a piece of work is executed, it is unique.

Hunting scene. This work demonstrates a clear tendency towards idealization.

Mastery of beauty and perspective in this mythological scene of Diana, goddess of the hunt. This work is executed using the bulino technique.

Detail of engraving on a lockplate. The storm is raging over a lake. The total absence of any frame or ornamentation allows the engraving to project itself beyond the confines of the space imposed by the shape of the weapon.

Detail on the underside of a gun: hunting scene engraved using the bulino technique.

Detail of engraving on the underside of a gun. The shading gives an impressive three-dimensional aspect to this mask inspired by ornaments of the Renaissance.

Engraving in progress, using the bulino technique.

Christian Freycon

France, 20th Century

Born at Saint-Etienne in 1931, Freycon took his first steps in engraving with his father, then attended the art school in Saint-Etienne under the direction of Professor Gadoud, who was considered the best of the French engravers in the 1950s. Freycon achieved the title of "Best Workman in France" in 1979. He gradually became something of an oddity within his genre because he never lost sight of the golden age of French engraving and its influence throughout the world. In fact it was by drawing inspiration from this tradition that Freycon developed his own creations, mastering all the techniques of engraving with impressive skill. His body of work is the manifestation of a professional, demanding and rigorous discipline. His lines, whether the finest, most delicate or deepest, are of exemplary clarity.

Engraving executed on a Granger shotgun, depicting 17th Century hunters. The chasing on the fences is beautiful. The butt is carved in the style of the first French Empire.

Balance of space and perspective in this hunting scene executed on a Granger gun.

Engraving, on a Granger gun, of a hunting scene in a landscape typical of the French countryside.

Exceptional engraving, on a Merkel rifle, of a cape buffalo in its surroundings.

Freycon created wonderful engravings and chasing work which recall those of the French Renaissance, and also engravings in Art nouveau and Art deco styles.
In contrast, he executed hunting scenes in 16th and 17th Century settings and costumes.
In the 1980s he innovated by engraving in abstract style. His works are often inlaid with different colored golds.
Christian Freycon had a close working relationship with the Granger firm of Saint-Etienne. He decorated hunting weapons for them which are considered among the most beautiful in the world. Alas, no man is a hero in his own country, and the vast majority of enthusiasts in France are no longer interested in such arms, a fact which the craftsmen of Saint-Etienne can only lament.
It is already a few years since Christian Freycon died. He did, however, leave us a further example of his immense talent: the creation of a splendid engraving that commemorates the bicentennial of the French Revolution, executed on a fine weapon made by Granger. The combination of these two astounding talents has brought about the creation of an exceptional decorative weapon.

This Granger shotgun commemorates the bicentennial of the French Revolution. The engraving was executed by Christian Freycon shortly before his death.

The lockplates and barrels are engraved with the flight to Varennes, a portrait of Marie-Antoinette as well as ...

... that of Louis XVI, and of course the storming of the Bastille. This marvel required seven hundred hours of work.

Christian Freycon has engraved the most beautiful weapons by Georges Granger and in particular this superb juxtaposition of lockplates in the style of Holland & Holland with barrels and fences that combines chasing and gold and platinum inlay inspired by the Renaissance.

Philippe Grifnée

Belgium, 20th Century

Born in 1952 at Verviers in Belgium, Grifnée followed the courses given by René Delcour at the armory school in Liège. Later, after setting up on his own, he produced engravings for the firms of Francotte and Lebeau-Courally, as well as for private collectors. Over time, his talent has gone from strength to strength and gunmakers such as Purdey and Holland & Holland now commission him to create engravings on weapons for the most important collectors in the world. To date, Grifnée has already produced around a hundred engravings for Holland & Holland. His reputation is becoming so considerable that the armory school in Liège, attended by students from all over the world, has asked him to teach engraving. Philippe Grifnée has succeeded in acquiring a wide range of experience in all the techniques of engraving firearms.

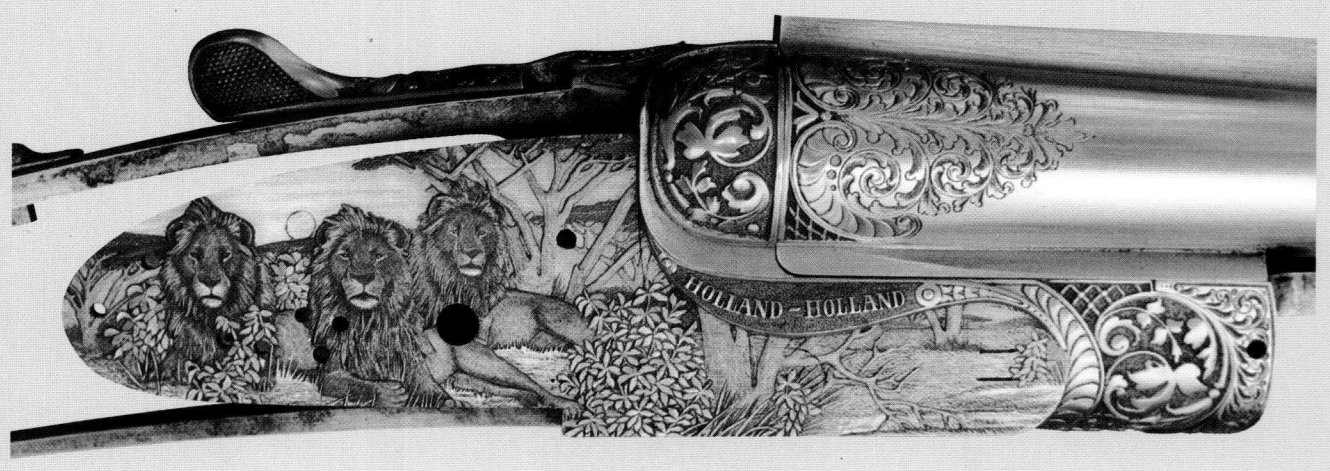

This decorative chasing of African wildlife (rhinoceros, buffalo and leopard), is executed on a recent Holland & Holland double Express rifle.

Opposite and left-hand page: animal scenes finely executed using the bulino technique and framed by superb chasing on a contemporary Holland & Holland double Express rifle.

Having created the design that he wishes to execute, Freycon engraves the outlines using a hammer and burin. Then, using the bulino technique, he shades in the backgrounds, flowers, leaves and scrolls in magnificent fashion. His characteristic style consists of leaving space within these settings to engrave highly evocative heads of dogs. He is also renowned for his mastery of inlay techniques using precious metals and for the animal scenes that he designs and engraves.

For Grifnée, who originally intended to go into clock-making, "engraving is my passion and the weapon is merely the medium".

Opposite and above: recent Holland & Holland bolt action rifle, completely inlaid with gold.

Above, opposite and below: engraving on a unique shotgun bearing the monogram of a prince. The inlay of pheasants is framed by delicate ornamentation.

Kenneth C. Hunt

***England,** 20th Century*

Born in 1935 at Weybridge in Surrey, Hunt is among the top gun engravers in the world. He is a professional at chasing, line-engraving, the bulino technique and at inlaying of precious metals. He has a wonderful way of executing compositions of a symbolic or mythological nature and places different colored golds into the surface of the steel using the dovetail technique. With burins and blunt scissors (tools for chiseling), he fashions the most beautiful high-reliefs. Also of note are the grotesque masks interspersed with decorations of acanthus leaves that harmoniously surround the mythological characters who themselves live in magical forests among imaginary animals and beings.

This type of scene, executed in a very pure and classic style, gives way to more contemporary compositions, illustrating the life of animals in an elegant and refined style. Through his work this artist portrays the image of a man walking in idyllic places, with his gun at his shoulder and his dog as his companion. Ken Hunt has engraved guns for leading world figures; including members of the English royal family. He is the undisputed master of English engravers and remains an international standard.

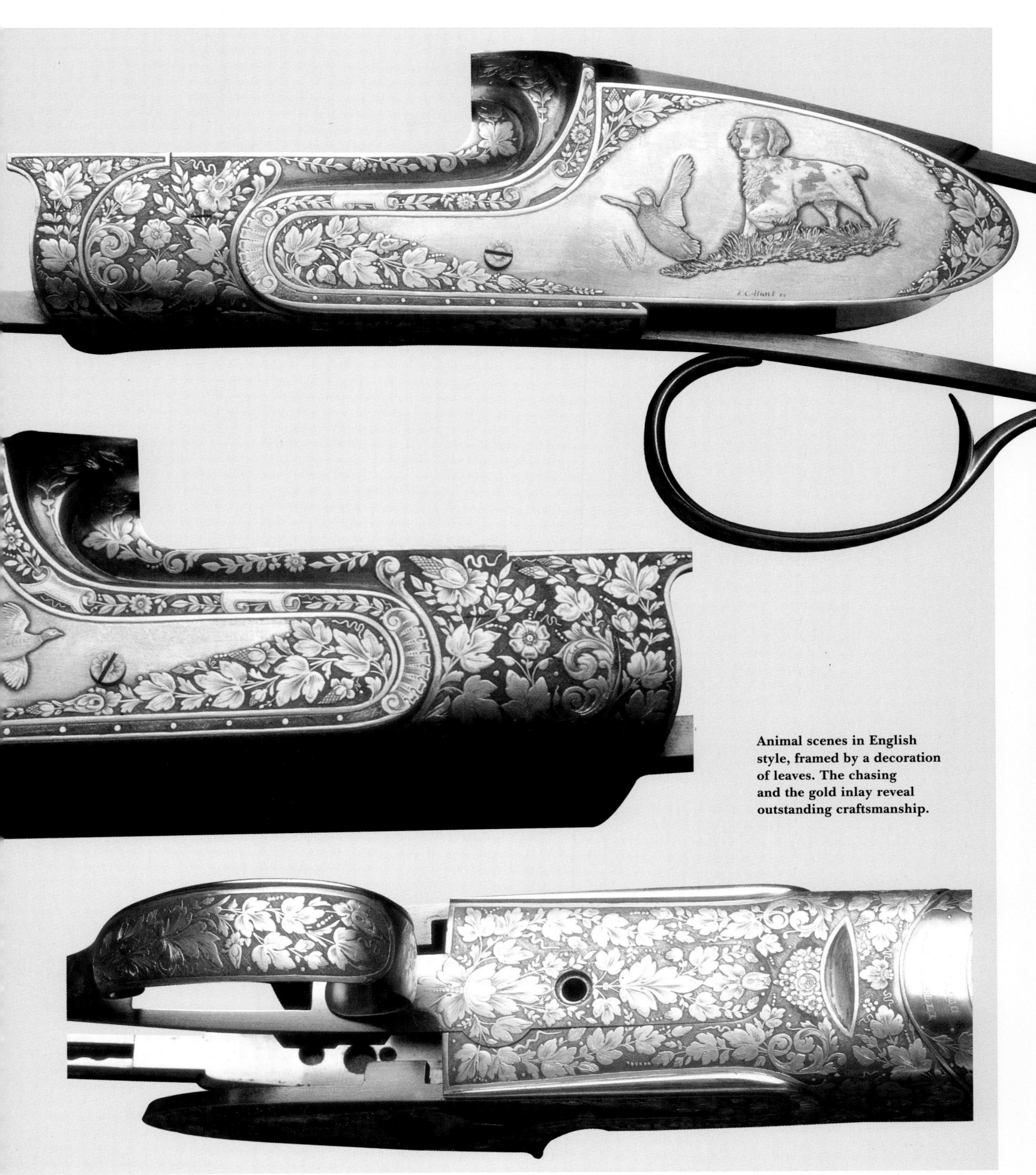

Animal scenes in English style, framed by a decoration of leaves. The chasing and the gold inlay reveal outstanding craftsmanship.

Alain Lovenberg

Belgium, 20th Century

Born in 1950 at Aisnes, in the Belgian Ardennes, Lovenberg attended the engraving courses at the armory school in Liège and rapidly proved himself to be one of the most promising students in his sector. An outstandingly gifted engraver, he creates highly personalized ornamental engravings in the Renaissance style. These engravings are executed on a recessed background with wonderful shading using the bulino technique. Sometimes his ornamentation is entirely chiseled: its quality and beauty are incomparable. Lovenberg is a legendary figure in the engraving world: he may, for example, refuse to carry out works whose sole function is to cover the maximum engraving space on a weapon for the minimum cost. In such a case he chooses to cultivate the land adjoining his farm instead.

This engraving is in the purest Empire style. It illustrates the Napoleonic epic and can be considered the masterpiece of the engraver Lovenberg. The animal scenes have been executed using the bulino technique and the chasing is outstandingly well controlled. The characters are inspired by the paintings of Géricault.

"Ambassadeur" double Express rifle with over/under barrels by Lebeau-Courally (Liège). The gold inlay is magnificently chased. The animal scene and decorations are extensively embellished in gold, but this original creation remains in good taste.

"Battue" double Express rifle with over/under barrels by Lebeau-Courally (Liège). The animals are engraved using the bulino technique; a good balance in the use of precious metals and steel for the ornaments.

The frame of this animal scene executed using line-engraving on a double Express rifle is superb. This work, inspired by Theodore Roosevelt's safari in 1909, was created by Lebeau-Courally for a film *(In the Blood)* which recounted this African expedition.

Gianfranco Pedersoli

Italy, 20th Century

Born in 1946 at Sarezzo, near Brescia, Pedersoli was, along with some other Italian engravers, a forerunner of modern engraving. He took his first steps in engraving with Giulio Timpini, head of the engraving workshop at Beretta, who allowed him to hone his skill in different techniques. He created engraving work in decorative, delicate English style, of floral-style bouquets and inlay work of precious metals. His meeting with Firmo Fracassi was the deciding factor in the development of his professional career. Highly impressed by the style and exceptional quality of Fracassi's engravings, Pedersoli concentrated on the execution of engravings which became increasingly sought after. As was bound to happen, Mario Abbiatico noticed him and offered him the opportunity to produce engravings that tested all his skills. Thanks to this long collaboration, Gianfranco Pedersoli refined the quality of his work and succeeded in finding his own style, consisting of ornaments made up of very long lines which intertwine in an often unexpected manner. Allowing room for spontaneity, Pedersoli likes to interweave acanthus leaves, flowers, and various species of birds and butterflies. These "dances of animals and plants" are tinged with a refined romanticism. The shading on the leaves, flowers and birds is very fine and delicate. The whole work, with the ornaments set against background shading of deepest

Splendid leopard engraved on a Beretta rifle. It is framed by original ornamentation created by the artist.

Marvelous grotesques created by the artist, engraved using the burin, hammer and hand graver. The absence of a border indicates the desire of the artist to project his work into space.

Gianfranco Pedersoli in his workshop. In all his work his technical and creative achievement stands out.

A highly romantic decoration created using the burin, hammer and hand graver on a Fabbri gun.

black, gives the impression of such considerable depth that the viewer may think he is looking at a low-relief sculpture. Gianfranco Pedersoli also creates evocative animal scenes, usually framed by highly elaborate decorations. In aquatic settings, the reeds are often enlarged in a surrealist manner, stretching their tapered leaves up into the air and over the water, creating shelters for the inhabitants of these idyllic landscapes. But peace does not last forever.

The unexpected appearance of hunters with their dogs disrupts these landscapes and brings them to life. In these scenes, however, the artist never expresses any violence.

Gianfranco Pedersoli studied the anatomy of the human body in great depth in order to create some magnificent engravings.

He created the neo-baroque style. In contrast, one can see in his work the influence of the technique of short lines and dots used by Firmo Fracassi. It should be pointed out that such engravings generally require several hundred hours of work. Nevertheless, people who do not have the means to treat themselves to such works but who admire them do sometimes approach Gianfranco Pedersoli. In such cases, he suggests engraving projects to them that are still unique but that require much less work, all the while meticulously maintaining a very high quality. As a result, with his passion and his creative talent, he has succeeded in creating at a lower cost engravings that are considered among the most beautiful.

Woodcock in flight and original ornamentation on an Abbiatico & Salvinelli sidelever double gun.

This Cosmi shotgun reveals the creative relationship that the artist maintains with the humanist spirit of the Renaissance.

Setter pointing partridges. Outstanding harmony between the landscape and the sober ornamentation.

Poetic and delicate hunting scene on a Piotti shotgun, depicting Diana, goddess of the hunt.

Giancarlo Pedretti

Italy, 20th Century

Born in 1949 at Gardone, Giancarlo Pedretti began his training in the 1960s. An excellent artist, he became an experienced professional.
He perfected the different techniques by working in the engraving shop at Beretta at the same period as Gianfranco Pedersoli, under the supervision of Giulio Timpini. It was also at this time that the grand master of engraving, Corombelle, created works for Beretta. Furthermore, Pedretti benefited from the experience of the ornamentation specialist M. Slatnik, an engraver of Austrian origin, and of other skilled professionals such as Baglioni and Tononcelli, who were also working with Beretta.
Later on, under the influence of Galeazzi and Fracassi, he began to learn the bulino technique (pushing the burin by hand). In the early 1980s, Giancarlo Pedretti created his own workshop. At first he worked for Abbiatico & Salvinelli and, over time, for all the foremost Italian firms. During these latter years, he has made his name with his animal engravings executed using the bulino technique. His style recalls the elegant English animal paintings of the 20th Century, although the flora that he creates has much greater contrast, and also evokes the natural landscapes of northern Italy. Pedretti possesses a talent for drawing portraits of animals and people

Engraving on a Bertuzzi gun (with hinged sideplates) of a dog holding a partridge in its mouth. Ornamentation in Renaissance style frames this engraving.

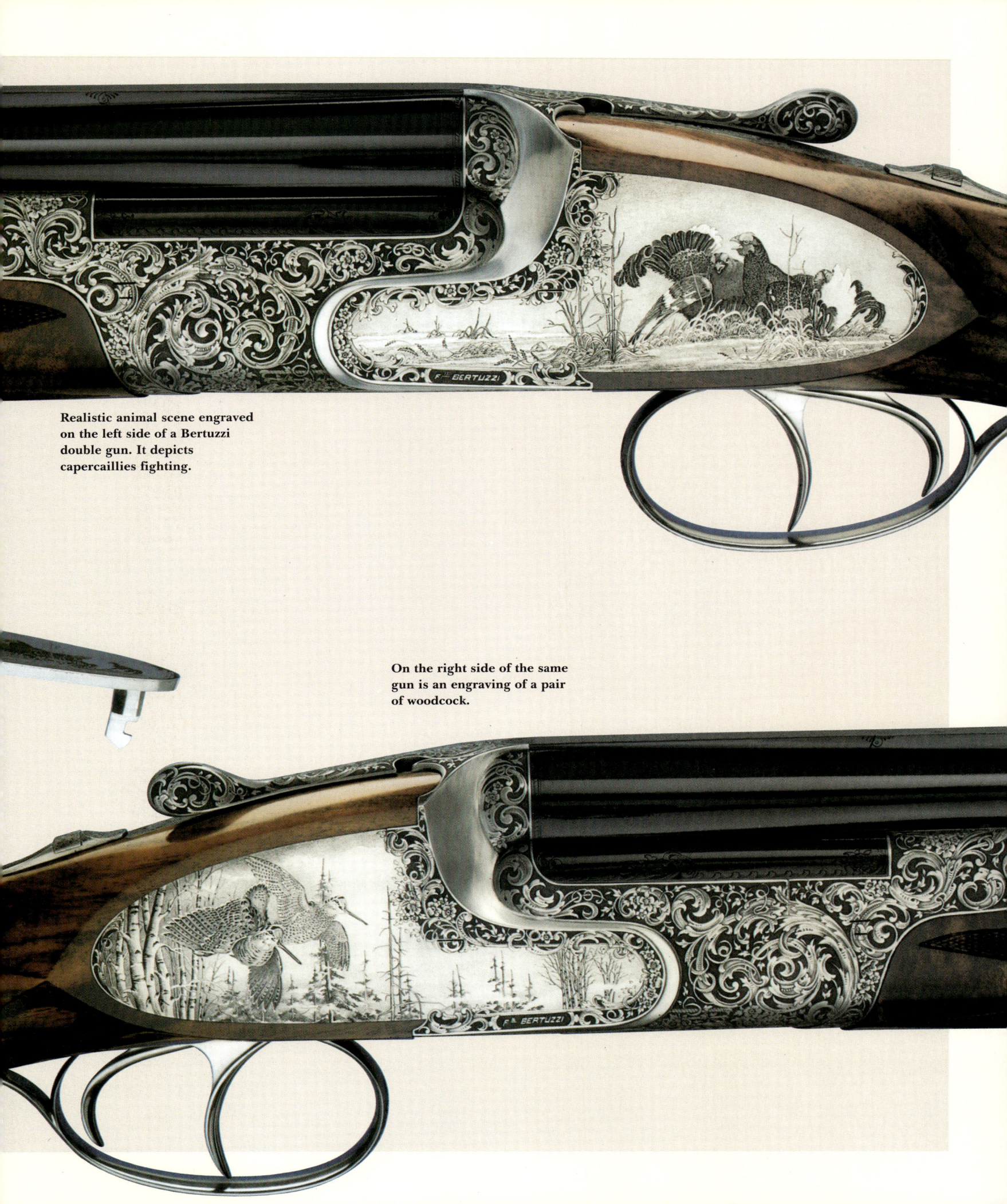

Realistic animal scene engraved on the left side of a Bertuzzi double gun. It depicts capercaillies fighting.

On the right side of the same gun is an engraving of a pair of woodcock.

or representations of architectural monuments, such as the famous Italian villas of the 16th Century by the Italian architect Andrea Palladio. In contrast, he succeeds brilliantly in the execution of Renaissance-style ornaments with recessed backgrounds adapted to his own taste, which he strews with magnificent bouquets of flowers inlaid with fine gold in different colors and delicately shaded to give them depth.

Nowadays, he creates engravings for Heym and for Purdey and other English and American firms.

He uses jewels to decorate hunting weapons and prestige knives. For all his engravings he first prepares a very precise drawing, then, once he has the agreement of the person commissioning the work, he executes the engraving. Today this artist is considered one of the innovators of Italian engraving of the last twenty years.

On a L. Bosis gun, beautiful ornamentation framing a mask and eagles inlaid with gold and shaded using the bulino technique.

Hunting scenes executed in magnificent style using the bulino technique on the lockplates of a L. Bosis shotgun.

Preparatory drawing for an engraving, together with its realization executed using the bulino technique on a L. Bosis gun.

Giovanni Bertella et Pietro Sabatti

Italy, 20th Century

Giovanni Bertella was born at Gardone, Val Trompia (Italy), in 1942. At around the age of seventeen he attended the music academy in Brescia, then he discovered engraving and learned the trade from the master, Baglioni. When he was twenty-one he started at Beretta as an engraver. It was there that he met Giulio Timpini. Pietro Sabatti was born in Brescia in 1941. After a professional stint in Geneva, first as an engraver of jewelry, then as a decorative designer and engraver with Piaget, he returned to Brescia, attracted by the revival of engraving in Italy, and made the acquaintance of Bertella.

Together with other engravers, he formed an engraving workshop and built up his contacts with Parisian gunmakers and engravers. After a collaboration with gunmakers in Paris, Bertella and Sabatti created an engraving workshop in rue Saint-Paul, Paris. They executed engravings for the top firms in Paris such as Gastinne, Renette, Callens et Mode, Jeannot and for a private clientele with a passion for creative engraving. In this workshop, they kept a space to display their creations. Bertella presented drawings of original animal engravings, and Sabatti displayed sculptures, figurative paintings engraved on metal plates and restorations of early arms. Bertella is famous for his creations of hunting scenes and original ornamentation. Bertella has returned to Italy and Sabatti still works in France.

View of a Piotti shotgun from above. The engraving and the extraordinarily delicate original ornaments are a creation of Giovanni Bertella.

Chasing inspired by the French Renaissance executed by Pietro Sabatti on a Piotti gun.

Chasing by Pietro Sabatti and engraving by Giovanni Bertella on a Browning double Express rifle.

Engraving inspired by Muslim art by Pietro Sabatti on a Cosmi shotgun. This engraving, executed in different colored steel, is inlaid with gold.

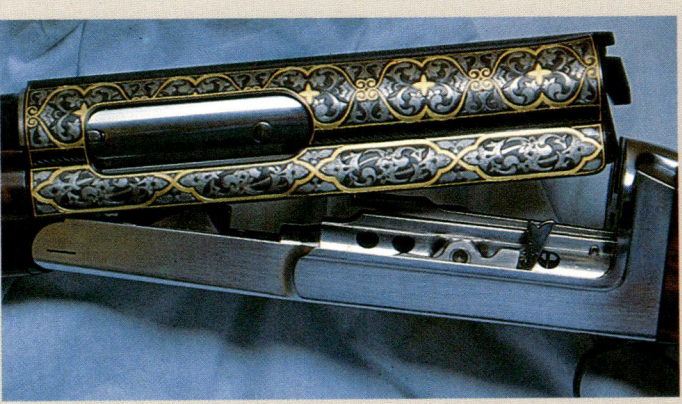

Allegorical scene engraved by Pietro Sabatti on a Piotti action and sideplates.

Manrico Torcoli

Italy, 20th Century

Born in 1954 at Gardone, Val Trompia, near Brescia in Italy, Manrico Torcoli worked for nine years as a metalsmith at the Beretta factory. He then tendered his resignation and took up engraving. He started out alone, armed only with his imagination, and concentrated on learning the bulino technique. Eventually he took his drawings and first attempts to Firmo Fracassi, who guided his early steps. Manrico Torcoli was quick to become something of a phenomenon, shattering the accepted criteria for engraving. His compositions were displayed on any surface that could be engraved. He thus succeeded in creating incredible animal scenes where different species of birds mingle, interspersed with the heads and bodies of dogs. Winged animals and an abundance of feathery ornamentation freely fill the space in a kind of magical dance which seems to go on forever. In other engravings the viewer is entranced by magnificent female nudes. Their perfect bodies are in a state of deep symbiosis with swans and other birds in a frenzied whirl of wings and feathers. It is also surprising to see the perspective of all these figures, and of the picture in general, deliberately turned upside-down and shattered, thus recalling certain aspects and outlines of compositions of animal figures found in prehistoric art.

This engraving expresses perfectly the sensitivity of the artist to the dramatic history of the American Indian. The figure in close-up is that of the Apache chief Geronimo. This engraving was executed on a Fabbri shotgun.

Wild horses engraved on a Fabbri gun. This is a technical feat when one considers the limits imposed by the shape of the weapon and its mechanism.

An engraving begun on a Fabbri gun for Steven Spielberg, on the theme of *Jurassic Park*.

Personal interpretation by Manrico Torcoli of the symbol of the American eagle. In his engravings, Torcoli often mixes female figures with animals.

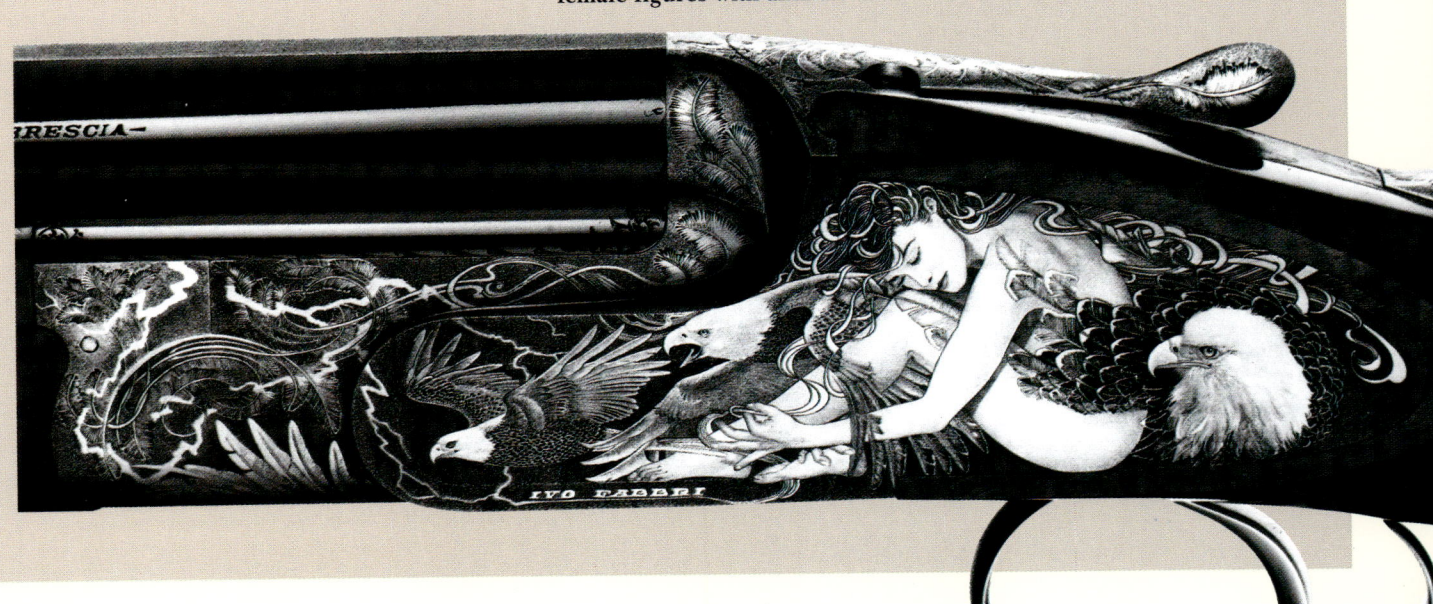

GLOSSARY

Ball: A single round projectile fired from a muzzleloader, whether smoothbore or rifled; as opposed to shot. The precursor of the modern bullet.

Bore: The longitudinal hole within a firearm's barrel; the caliber, i.e. diameter, of that hole; or the size, or gauge, of a gun expressed in the number of lead balls of that diameter that would add up to a pound (as in a 12-bore or 20-bore gun).

Breech: The rear of a firearm barrel (as opposed to its muzzle); the chamber is within the breech.

Breechloader: A firearm that can be loaded from the rear of its barrel(s), a much more convenient and quicker method than loading via the muzzle, but one that requires superior technology because of the need to lock the breech against the detonation of the cartridge.

Bulino: In Italian, the hand tool, or graver, with which the engraver cuts his designs into metal. Also a particular style of engraving, characteristically Italian, in which images are created with minute cuts and dots instead of scribed lines, creating the halftone effect of a black-and-white photograph.

Bullet: A single projectile fired from a breechloading rifle. Whereas a ball is round, a bullet is conical.

Burin: An engraver's tool that is driven with a hammer.

Caliber: The nominal bore diameter of a firearm, expressed in thousandths of an inch (e.g., .256) or in millimeters (e.g., 6.5mm).

Cartridge: A one-piece load for a firearm, with the bullet, powder and primer held within a shell. The evolution of breechloading firearms depended upon the simultaneous development of the self-contained cartridge.

Centerfire: A type of cartridge that has its primer set in the center of the base of the shell (as opposed to rimfire). This allows a shell to be reloaded (essentially remanufactured) more easily.

Chamber: The portion of a barrel that houses the powder and projectile when ready to be fired; the inside of the breech.

Chasing: Carving of metal, whether in low or high relief.

Choke: An internal constriction within the barrel of a shotgun, near the muzzle, that concentrates the spread of the shot pattern downrange.

Copperplate: A delicate engraving technique that calls for light cuts or lines in the metal.

Damascening: A superficial decorative design or pattern etched, inlaid or otherwise applied onto steel; not to be confused with damascus.

Damascus: A type of metal made up of alternate layers of steel and iron that have been forge-welded (hammered under high heat) together into a single piece. In the 19th Century, strips of damascus steel were spiral-wound around mandrels and forged into gun barrels that were notably light yet strong, as well as beautiful, because of the pattern created by the alternating layers.

High-quality damascus barrels were extremely labor- and skill-intensive to make and were declared obsolete as soon as metallurgy and machining technology had progressed enough to let barrelmakers produce similarly thin-walled, straight tubes of ingot steel at a lower price.

Express: A term applied to high-velocity rifle cartridges beginning in 1856 by London gunmaker James Purdey, who wished to compare his new rifles (developed for the dangerous game of India and Africa) to the high-speed "Express" trains that were then also new in England.

Firing Pin: The part of a modern firearm's action that is driven by the hammer against the primer in order to ignite the powder in the cartridge. With the Lefaucheux system, each cartridge had its own firing pin.

Flintlock: A type of firearm, or its ignition system, that relies on sparks created by a piece of flint striking a steel to light the priming powder that then ignites the main charge in the chamber. This was a great improvement over the wheellock and was in turn supplanted by the percussion lock.

Fuselock: The first ignition system that allowed guns to be hand-held (instead of mounted on caissons or swivels). A burning length of fuse, or match, is clamped in the gun's serpentine, or hammer; pulling the trigger brings the fuse into contact with the priming powder, which in turn ignites the main powder charge in the chamber. Also known as a matchlock.

Gauge: See Bore.

Graver: An engraver's tool that is pushed by the hand (as opposed to a burin).

Gun: Loosely used to mean any firearm, but in fact one with a smooth (non-rifled) barrel; a shotgun, as opposed to a rifle or pistol.

Hammer: That part of a firearm's works, usually spring-loaded, which strikes the firing pin or cartridge primer, to fire the round.

Hammerless: A type of firearm in which the hammer is enclosed within the action and is cocked, or brought into firing position, mechanically; as opposed to a hammergun, with external hammers that are usually cocked by hand. The hammer of a "hammerless" firearm is often called a tumbler.

Inlay: A decorative technique that involves cutting into the base metal or wood and filling the incision with another material, often gold or silver (in metal) or ivory, mother of pearl or horn (in wood).

Intaglio: A decorative technique that consists of removing the background around ornaments in order to make them stand out more prominently.

Lefaucheux System: An early (invented 1836) type of breechloading ammunition that featured a pin protruding from the rim of the metallic cartridge, which when loaded into a firearm stuck up through a slot in the breech. The hammer strikes the pin, driving it into and igniting the priming powder, which is contained within the cartridge case. Also known as pinfire. Named for the inventor, Casimir Lefaucheux, and significant because it was the first system that provides a satisfactory seal against the gases generated by the detonating powder.

Lock: That part of a firearm's works, or action, which includes the hammer and its spring and which fires the round when the trigger is pulled.

Lockplate: A metal plate to which is attached a sidelock firearm's lock. Also known as a sideplate.

Marquetry: A decorative technique that consists of completely covering a base material with other materials for ornamental purposes.

Matchlock: See fuselock.

Muzzle: The tip, or front, of the barrel of a firearm; the opposite of the breech.

Muzzleloader: A type of firearm that must be loaded from the muzzle; the powder charge, a retaining wad, the ball or shot and then another wad are tamped down into the chamber with a long ramrod; made obsolete by the breechloader.

Percussion Lock: A type of ignition system, used primarily for muzzleloading firearms, pioneered by Alexander Forsyth and Samuel Pauly early in the 19th Century. Flint and steel eventually were replaced by a copper cap, containing a small priming explosive, which is press-fit onto a hollow nipple threaded into the breech of the barrel. When this cap is struck by the hammer, the primer ignites the main charge. This is far faster, more reliable and weatherproof than the flintlock system, and many flintlock weapons were eventually converted to percussion-fire.

Pinfire: See Lefaucheux.

Primer: The small charge exploded by a firearm's hammer, which in turn ignites the main charge that propels the ball, shot or bullet. In muzzleloading weapons, the primer was fine-grain loose powder (which was poured into a special pan) or a percussion cap. In modern breechloading firearms, the primer is contained within the base of the cartridge.

Relief: The three-dimensional aspect of chasing, carving or intaglio. In low relief, the background has been removed to a moderate degree; high relief approaches sculpture, where the subject appears nearly in the round.

Rimfire: A type of cartridge that has its primer contained within the rim of the rear of the shell. A rimfire shell is not reloadable and typically is used only for inexpensive low-power, low-pressure cartridges such as the .22 Short, Long, Long Rifle and Magnum.

Rifle: A firearm with grooves cut helically along its bore. These grooves make the ball or bullet spin, which stabilizes it in flight and greatly improves its accuracy and ballistic performance; as opposed to a smoothbore.

Rifling: The grooves in the bore that distinguish a rifle.

Round: One shot or cartridge, whether bullet, ball or shot.

Sidelock: A type of lock that is fastened to the side of a firearm, where it is easily accessible, as opposed to, for example, a boxlock that is inside the action.

Sideplate: See Lockplate.

Screwplate: In a single-barrel sidelock firearm, a plate on the stock opposite the lockplate that is threaded to accept the screws that fasten the lockplate.

Shell: The container portion of a cartridge, typically brass (for a rifle) or paper or plastic (for a shotgun), which holds the powder, primer and bullet or shot. When a round is fired, the empty shell must be extracted from the chamber before the weapon can be reloaded.

Shot: Small pellets, generally made of an alloy of lead, fired in a cluster from a shotgun; as opposed to a ball or bullet.

Shotgun: A smoothbore gun that fires shot and generally is used for wingshooting, i.e. shooting birds or clay targets in flight, or occasionally for small, fast game such as rabbits or squirrels; as opposed to a rifle.

Smoothbore: A firearm with no rifling in its bore; not necessarily a shotgun, for it may be used to fire a ball.

Stock: The part(s) of a firearm that hold the barrel, action and other metal components. Some unusual presentation stocks have been made of materials such as ivory, and some modern stocks are molded of light, weather-resistant synthetics, but stocks usually are wood, and that wood usually is walnut. Many firearms require two-piece stocks: a forend and a buttstock.

Wheellock: An early type of ignition system that relies on sparks created by a flint that is brought into contact with a revolving steel wheel. The spring that powers the wheel is wound by the shooter, in advance, with a special key. This was an evolution of the fuselock and preceded the flintlock

BIBLIOGRAPHY

C. GAIER, *Five Centuries of Arms Making* in Liège, Liège, 1996

J. GRABOWSKA, "The Decoration of Firearms," in *Pollard's History of Firearms*, publ. C. BLAIR, Feltham, 1983, pp. 478-508.

S.V. GRANCSAY, *Master French Gunmakers' Designs of the XVII-XIX Centuries*, New York, 1970.

J.F. HAYWARD, *Antique Firearms: 1500-1600*, Fribourg, 1963; *1660-1830*, Fribourg, 1964.

T. LENK, *The Flintlock: Its Origin and Development*, London, 1965.

R.L. WILSON, *Steel Canvas, The Art of American Arms*, 1995.

INDEX

Page numbers in italics refer to photographs

A

Abbiatico & Salvinelli 119, *126*, 148
Abbiatico & Salvinelli double *114*, *146*
Abbiatico (Mario) 113, 114, *115*, *126*, 144
action 93, 94, 103, 109
Aisne 140
Alexander VI (Pope) 9
"Ambasadeur" double Express by Lebeau-Corally *142*
America 73, 74
Amsterdam 51, 68
Androuet du Cerceau (Jacques) 41
Angers 62
Anson (system) 107
Anson and Deeley 19
Anson and Deeley (system) 93, 107
appliqué *72*
Aquafresca (Matteo) 66
Aquafresca (Sébastien) 66
Arault (Jacques Louis) 53
arquebus 11, 12, 13, 21
arquebus (external wheellock) *14*, *38*
arquebus (fuselock) *12*, *13*
arquebus (internal wheellock) *58*
arquebus (wheellock) 7, *13*, *35-36*, *37*, *37*, *40*, *43*, 44
Artois (Count of) 53
August II 60
Austria 117, 119

B

Baerten 117
Baglioni 148, 152
Baker (David J.) 95
Baker (Samuel) 8
Baltic (countries) 45
bar-action lock *105*
Bargi 66
barrel 12, 15, 20, 34, *37*, 40, 44, 50, 52, 57, 60, *63*, *65*, *71*, 73, *89*, 110
  damascus 16, *17*, *19*, *71*, *79*, *81*, *89*, *101*
  machine-bored 17
  over and under 20, 101
  side by side *55*
  sliding 19
  smoothbore 11, *38*, *43*
  solid-steel 17
  tilting 19
Basque (country) 71
Bastille *133*
Battista (Michele) *64*, 67
"Battue" double Express by Lebeau-Corally *142*
bayonet 7
Beckers 68
Behr 68
Belgium 88, 100, 116, 134, 140
Berain (Jean) 49, 66
Beretta 22, 26, 112, *112*, 116, *118*, 119, 144, *144*, 148, 152, 154
Beretta over/under *114*, *127*
Berleur 69
Berlin 98
Bernard *19*, *79*, *81*
Bernard (Léopold) 82, *84*
Bernard (Nicolas) 82
Bertella (Giovanni) 116, 152, *153*
Bertuzzi 119, *148*, *149*
big game hunting 17
Biron 69
blacking 29
blueing 28
blunderbuss 29
Bologna 40, 65, 66
Bonaparte *126*, *127*
Bonaparte (Jérôme) 16
Bongarde (Armand) 60
Borovnik (Ludwig) 117, 119
Bosis 119, *124*, *150*, *151*
Boss 107
Boussart (Joseph) *79*, 90, *90*
Boutet (Nicolas-Noël) *26*, 55, *55*, *56*, 57
Boutet (style) 63, 71
bow 7
breech 12, 16, 17, 18, 71, *98*, *50*, *52*, *80*, *82*, *89*
breechloading 19
Breidenfelter (Johann Paul) 60
Brescia 39, 40, 64, 65, 126, 144, 152, 154
Brown 117
Browning *21*, *117*
Browning A5 *113*
Browning double Express *153*
Bry (Théodore de) 66
bulino *23*, 110, *111*, 124, *127*, *128*, *129*, *135*, 140, *141*, *142*, *150*, *151*, 154
bullet box 74
burin 22, *22*, *23*, *24*, *26*, 124, 126, *138*, *145*
burnisher *23*, *23*
butt 14, 30, 38, 41, *42*, 45, 50, 51, 52, 54, *54*, 58, *58*, 60, 67, *72*, 74, 108, *130*
  "claw" 44, *44*, 45
  "cow's hoof" *51*
  "duck bill" 88
  "French head" *56*, 71, 82
  "ham" style 14, 50
  "Madrid" style 64, 70, 71
  "pétrinal" 14, 41
  Catalan 70
  fishtail 7, 14, 39, 41
  fluted 71
  spiral 14
  plate *60*
  pad 51
Buxton (Edward) 8

C

Campanelli 124
carbine - fourteen barrel *62-63*
carbine - wheellock 12, 44
carbine - Winchester *98-99*
carbine - with short barrel *56-57*
Caron (Alphonse) *83*, 86
cartridge (centerfire) 19
cartridge (pinfire) 19
Castellesi (Adriano) 9
Catalonia 71
Chapuis (Paul) 119
Chapuis Armes 119
Charles the Fifth *10*
chasing 24, 26, *26*, 38, 39, 41, 43, 50, 56, 59, 60, *64*, 65, 73, 84, *85*, 92, 94, *101*, 103, 106, *117*, 124, 126, *130*, 132, *133*, 138, *139*, *141*
chasing tool 23, 138
Chaucer 109
cheekpiece *33*, 38, *61*, 82
Chiring 119
chiselwork *107*
Churchill 107
Claesen (Charles) 90, *91*, 101
Claudin (Fernand) 86
Cloes (J. J.) *80*, 91
Coggan (Philip) 117, 122
Collinet (Charles) 91
Colt 98
Colt (Eugène) 97
Colt (Oscar) 97
comb 54, 74
Cominazzo (Lazaro) 40
Compiègne 7
Conrad (F.) 97
Cordier Daubigny (Philippe) 43
Corombelle (Hippolite) *112*, 117, 148
Corombelle (Lyson) *112*, 117
Cortisi 119
Cosmi *146*, *153*
Coster (Cornelis) 68
Courally (Ferdinand) 95
Cranach (Lucas) 10
Creative Art 124, 125
crossbow 7, 9, *9*, 10, *10*
cutter *27*
Cuvelier *19*, 91
Czarniecki (Stephan) 103
Czechoslovakia 44

D

Daisenberger (Bartolomeus) 61
damascening 28, *28*, 35, 41, 50, 55, 56, 79, 100, 101, *101*
damascus 17, 82
Danse (Jean-Joseph) 91
Davydov (Nikita) 45
De La Pierre 68
De Lacollombe 53
De Marteau (Gilles) 53
De Marteau (Joseph) 53
De Sainte (Pierre) 53
decorations 16
Delaune (Étienne) 36, 41
Delcour (René) 134
Delvenne (Alphonse) 93, 112
Desenzani 119
Devillers 68, 69
Devillers (Joseph) 88, *89*
Devisme 17
Dickson 107, *107*
dog *79*, *83*
Dolep (Andrew) 62
Donnay (Lambert) 91
double percussion 89
double-barrel *101*
double-barrel 12 bore hammerless 94
double-barrel Express *116*
double barrel over and under 92
double-barrel percussion shotgun *80*, 88
double-barrel with sliding barrels 20
double-barreled 16, 20, *83*, *84*, 93
double-barreled flintlock 16, 53
double shotgun for pinfire cartridges *78*
Dresden 60
Drilling 16
Droogbrood (Wernand) 69
Dumoulin 118
Dupe (William) 62
Dupré (Augustin) 57
Durut *51*
Düsseldorf 60

E

Egypt 126
Eibar 71
embellishments 55, 56
embossing punch 23
England 54, 100, 106, 107, 122, 138
engraving 22, 35, 103
engraving - copperplate *23*, *24*, 25, 54, 57, *85*, 92, 94, 138, 143
engraving - English 93, *108*, 109
engraving - English bouquet 95, *109*
engraving - intaglio 20, 23, *24*, *27*, *34*, *36*, 59, 65, 66, 84, 85, *92*, 94, 95, 97, 100, *117*, 124, 125, 140
engraving - relief 92
engraving - shallow-cut 96, 97
engraving - tapestry *106*
Erttel (Andreas) 60
etching 26, 59, *91*
etching - dry-point 23, *23*
Express 19, *117*

F

Fabbri 119, *145*, *154*, *155*
Falloise (Joseph) 90, 91
Falloise (Louis) 91
Fausti (Giacomo) 124
Fedorovitch (Michel) 45
fence 93
Ferlach 117, 119
Ferraglio (Severino) 23
file 23
Fils (André) 31, 87
finger-rest 13
firearm - automatic 20
fittings 40, 69
Flachat (Jérôme) *101*
flint 67
flintlock 15, 17, 18, 43, 50, *51*, *52*, *54*, 55, 58, *60*, *63*, *64*, *71*, *72*, 74
flintlock repeater 66
Florence 10
Fontainebleau 7
Ford (Gerald) 21
forend 108, *114*
foresight 51
fork 23
Forsyth (Alexander John) 18
Fracassi (Firmo) 114, *126*, 144, *146*, 148, 154
France 7, 9, 41, 43, 48, 57, 60, 70, 82, 88, 100, 117, 119, 130
François I 9, 21, 36
Francotte (Auguste) 92, 118, 134
Frappier (Joseph) 53
Frederick I of Sweden 47, 73
French gray 28, *29*
Freycon (Christian) 117, *130*, 132
frizzen 15, *64*
Funken (Félix) *113*, 117
furnishings 17, 109
fuse powder 13, 14
fuselock 12, 13

G

Gadoud (Professor) 130
Galeazzi (Angelo) 114, *115*, 148
Gardone 40, 152, 154
Gauvain (Alfred) 86
Geffrois 119
Gelderland 9
George II 62
Gerhard (Adam Anton) 47
Géricault *141*
German Empire 10, 11, 13
Germany 7, 37, 39, 72, 119
Geronimo 154
gilding 28, 50, 54, 56, 58, 82, 94
Gillot (Claude) 53
Giovanelli (Cesare) 115, 116, 124
Gomes (Bartolomeu) 71
Granger *130-131*, *132*, *133*
Granger (George) 119, *133*
Granger (house of) *132*
Grant 107
graver 22, 24, 26, 110, *145*
Great Britain 8, 57, 62, 94
Grifnée (Philippe) *111*, 117, 134, 136
grip 42, 88, 93, 94, 97, 108
Guélard 49
Guérard (Nicolas) 53

H

Haaken-Plondeur *80*
Hadley (Henry) *63*
hallmark 60, *71*
hammer 14, 15, 16, *22*, 24, *44*, 52, 54, 58, *63*, *64*, 77, 82, *105*, 124, *145*
  external 19, 38
  fancy 85
  flint 18
  internal 19
  striking 18
  swan-neck 50
"hammerless" sidelock 107
hammerless (system) 107
hand-guard 75, 97
hand-rest 92
Hartford 97
Hartmann & Weis 119
Helfricht (Cuno A.) 98
Henequin (Jean) 41
Henri IV 41
Henry VIII 9
Herculaneum 54

Herman (Jean) 91
Heym 150
Holland 9
Holland & Holland 94, 107, *110, 111,* 122, *123, 133,* 134
Holland & Holland bolt action *136*
Holland & Holland double Express *135*
Holland & Holland Express 21
Holy Roman Empire 37, 43
Honoré (Charles) 90
hounds (hunting with) 6, *10*
Hudson (Thomas) *63*
Huet (C.) 49
Hunt (Kenneth) 138
hunting with arquebus *34*

I
immersion 29
inlay 26, 27, 27, 30, *33,* 35, 39, 41, *42, 43,* 44, 52, *56,* 57, 58, *64,* 65, 73, 75, *80,* 84, *85,* 97, 103, 106, *133,* 136, *137, 139, 142*
Italy 7, 39, 43, 66, 112, 114, 119, 124, 126, 144, 148, 152, 154

J
Jachimek (Jan) 101, *102*
Jacquinet (Claude) 49
Johan Georg I 8
Johan Georg II 8
Jones (Inigo) 62
Joseph I *71*
Julin (Nicolas) 90

K
Keiser (Georg) 60
Kentucky 74, 75
Kentucky type *75*
key (wheellock) *14*
knife (hunting) 7
Kolbe 62
Kölderer (Jörg) 9
Kosciuszko (Tadeusz) *103*

L
La Marre (Jacques) 60
Lacollombe *68*
Lancaster (Charles) 107
Laroche (Jean Baptiste) 53
Lasonder 68
Le Blon (Michel) 41
Le Bourgeois (Marin) 43
Le Bourgeois (Pierre) 43
Le Couvreux (Jean) 50
Le Hollandois 49, *67*
Le Page *54,* 57
Le Prévost (Hubert) *41*
Lebeau-Corally 118, *119,* 134, *143*
Lebeda (Antoine) 90
Lebeda (Anton Vincent) 100
Lebeda (Anton) 100, *101*
Lebeda (Ferdinand) 90, 100, *101*
Lebeda Brothers *91*
Lefaucheux 27, 87, *90*
Lefaucheux (Casimir) 18
Lefaucheux (system) 18, *19, 78, 84*
Leipzig 90
Lejeune *68*
Lemaître (Léon) 91, 92, *93*
Lepage-Moutier 87
Libaerts (Eliseus) 44
Liège 10, 44, 53, 56, 68, 69, 81, 88, 90, 92, 134, 140
Liénard 86, 90, *91*
Lisbon 71
lockplate *16,* 38, 40, 44, 49, 50, 51, *56, 58, 63,* 71, 73, *80,* 94, *95,* 101, *101, 111, 126, 127, 129, 133, 151*
lockplate - "miquelet" 70, *71*
lockplate - false *67*
lockplate - internal wheellock *59*
lockplate - Madrid 70
London 62, 81, 86
Lorenzoni (Michele) 66
Lorris (Guillaume de) 109

Louis XIII *8,* 40, 41
Louis XIV 6, 48, 52, 53, 57, 68
Louis XV 6, *52,* 57, 68
Louis XVI 6, 53, *54,* 68, 93
Louis-Philippe *83, 86*
Louroux 68
Lovenberg (Alain) 25, 117, 140, *141*
Lucas (J-F.) 57

M
Maastricht 68
Madrid 71
Manufrance 119
Marcou (François) 49, *67*
Marie-Antoinette 6, *133*
Markland 17
Marly-le-Roi 7
marquetry 30, *33*
Maryland 73
Massin 68
Maximilian (Emperor) 9
Medici (Cosimo de') 10
Medici (Francesco) 114, *114*
Menichetti (L.) 20
Merkel *131*
Meung (Jean de) 109
Michelangelo 124
Monlong (Pierre) 62
Mountbatten (Lord) *123*
mountings *20,* 50, 60, 71, 75, *80, 89, 92*
Munich 59, *61*
musket (flintlock) 73
musket (fuselock) *39*
muskets (hunt with) *11*
muzzle 12, 16, 17, 35, 50, 52

N
Napoleon I 6, *54,* 56, 88
Napoleon III 92, 94
Neer Eglon (Hendrick van der) *69*
"Nemrod" double-barrel by Lebeau-Courally 119
Nero (palace of) 35
Netherlands 39, 44, 68, 88
New Haven 97
New York 96
Nies (Joseph) 60
Nimschke (Louis D.) 96, *98*
Niquet (Claude) 68, *68*
North Carolina 73
Nüremburg 9, 51

O
Obiltschnig (Hans) 117
ornaments *95*
Oudry (Jean-Baptiste) 57
over and under barrels 21

P
Palladio (Andrea) 62, 150
pan *64*
Paris 62, 81, 88, 90, 91
Pauly (Samuel) 18
Pedersoli (Gianfranco) 115, 144, 146, 148
Pedretti (Giancarlo) 115, 148
Peli (Valerio) 124
Pennsylvania 73
Penterman 68
percussion *31, 86,* 86, 87
percussion lock 18, 57
Périn 119
Peter the Great 72
Petrovna (Elisabeth) 73
Pfintzing (Melchior) 9
Piardi (Armando) 124
pike 7
pinfire cartridges (for) 18, 19, 31
Piotti *116, 118,* 119, *121, 124, 125, 147, 152, 153*
Pirmet *16,* 28
plate *49, 91*
plate (base of) *54*
Poland 44, 45, 60
Pombal (Marquis de) *71*

Pompeii 54
Portugal 70, 71
Potgisser 91
Pottet 19
powder flask 12, *64*
powder pan 13, 16, 14, 18
powder pan cover 15
Prague 59, 90, *91*
Pramesberger 119
primer 18
Puiforcat (Pierre) 53
Pulaski (Casimir) *102*
punch 43
Purdey 19, 95, *105, 106,* 107, *108,* 115, 134, 150
Purdey & Sons 94
pusher *27*

R
Raick (Mathieu) 88
Rambert 90
Rapp (Count) 56, 57
Redon 119
Renkin (Jean-Toussaint) 69
Renneson 57
Reynier (Adrien) 49
rifling 13
Ripamonti 119
Ripoll 71
Rizzini 119
Robert 18
Rome 40, 65
Ronchard and Cizeron 86, 87
Rongé Brothers 77
Roosevelt (Theodore) 8, *143*
Russia 45, 72, 103

S
Sabatti (Pietro) 152, *153*
Sadeler 44
safety catch 93
Saint-Étienne 53, 81, *86,* 87, *101,* 130, 132
Saint-Germain-en-Laye 7
Salvinelli 113
Salzburg 58
Sarezzo 144
Savin 119
Saxony 60
screwplate 50, *51,* 52, *52,* 56, 59, 60, 66, 68, 72, 73
Selous (Frederick) 8
serpentine 13
Sforza (Cardinal) 9
shading *129,* 144
shadow 110, *127*
side by side Boss *109*
side by side Woodward & Sons double *107*
sidelock 107, *112*
sideplate *20,* 40, 52, *64, 89, 92,* 93, 103, 109
sight bead 51
Silesia 44
Simonin (Claude) 48, 50, 51
Simonin (Jacques) 51
Singer (Johann) 117
Slatnik 148
Sosnowski *102*
Spain 70, 71
Spielberg (Steven) 155
Springfield 97
St. Petersburg 73
Steduto (Giovanni) 124
stock *31,* 38, 41, 50, *51, 56,* 57, *57,* 59, 68, 70, 71, 73, 74, *80,* 81, 82, *85,* 86, *89,* 93, 100, 101, *101,* 103, *103,* 110, *114*
Stradanus 10, *11, 34, 37*
Straeten (Jan van der) 10
Switzerland 11
sword 7

T
Talenti (Ugo) 124
temper 28, 109
Terzi 115

Thiermay 68
Thornton (Thomas) 62
Thuraine *49, 67*
Thuringia 7, *14*
Thys (Marcel) 118
Timipini (Giulio) *115,* 116, 144, 148, 152
Tinlot (Jean-Michel) 31, 91, 92
tip of the ramrod 51
Tivoli (park) 9
Tononcelli 148
Torcoli (Manrico) 115, 154, *155*
Toschi 119
Toula 72, 73, 103
tracing wheel 23
Trajan (baths of) 35
trap shooting 8
trigger 13, 15, 16, 17, *64,* 79
trigger-guard *19,* 26, 51, *56,* 79, *80, 83,* 92, *93,* 103
tschinke 44, 45, *45*

U
Ulrich (John) 97
Umbria *67*
United States 8, 96, 103
Utrecht 68

V
Varennes (flight to) *133*
venery 7, 8
Venice 40
Vernet (Carle) 6
Verney-Carron 119
Verviers 134
Vienna 58, 59, 60
Vierling 16
Virginia 73
Vrancken (Louis) 116, *117*

W
Waroux (Joseph) 91, 92
Warsaw 101, *102*
Watrin (André) 117
Watteau 124
weapon - percussion hunting *102*
weapon - wheellock 59
Westley-Richards 107
wheellock *12, 14, 33, 34,* 58, *61*
William III 62
Winchester 97, *96*
Woodward 107

Y
Young (Gustave) 97

Z
Zanotti 119
Zelner (Kaspar) 58
Zuloaga (Placido) 90

PHOTOGRAPHIC CREDITS

All the photographs are by **Fanny Bruno,**
with the exception of:

Beretta Archives: 113 (top)
Boulay, Hervé: 21 (top), 104 to 109
Coggan Archives: 122, 123
Creative Art Archives: 124, 125
Daehnhardt, Rainer: 70-71
Dufays, Luc: 140 to 143
Fracassi Archives: 126 to 129
Freycon Archives: 130 to 133
Galeazzi Archives: 114 (top), 115 (top right), 116 (left)
Grifnée Archives: 134 to 137
Herstal S.A. Archives: 113 (bottom)
Holland & Holland Archives: 110, 111
Humbert, Christian: 98, 99
Lovenberg Archives: 25 (bottom)
Pedersoli Archives: 144, 145 (top, right, bottom), 146, 147
Pedretti Archives: 148, 149, 150
Sabatti Archives: 116 (top), 152, 153
Torcoli Archives: 154, 155

Museum of Arms, Liège: 68, 74, 75, 90, 91, 112, 117 (bottom)
Army Museum, Paris: 44-45 (top)
Museum of Hunting / Matheus: 13, 32, 33, 38, 39, 40, 44,
44-45 (middle), 51, 52, 54, 60, 61, 67 (bottom), 73
RMN: 11; R.G. Ojeda 69

D.R.: 8, 10, 12, 18, 34 (top), 41, 48, 49, 50, 63 (bottom), 72, 115 (top left)

This edition published by
KNICKERBOCKER PRESS
276 Fifth Avenue, Suite 206
New York, NY 10001
First English language edition, 1999
© Copyright, Paris, 1998

All rights reserved. No part of this publication may be reproduced
or transmitted in any form or by any means, electronic or mechanical,
including photocopy, recording or any other information storage
and retrieval system, without prior permission in writing from the publisher.

ISBN: 1-57715-087-2

Printed in Spain